Connally Gilliam's unflinching honesty ab... ...m personal
journey and struggles for her own d... ...timony that
temporarily closed doors m... ...uch more!
Our attitudes def... ...ism
of a half-full or h... ...i is
ab...

C... ...N
Investiga... ...urnalist and author of
Shattered Innocence—The Millennium Holocaust

This book is not just for those of us who, for now, remain
unintentionally single, but for anyone struggling with a deep
restlessness for that "good something"—whatever it may be—that they
long for, strive for, and hope will become a reality in this life.

KRISTEN BUCHER
Lawyer, Washington, DC

Miss Gilliam opens up realistically how the Christian life may need
to be lived out by an increasing number of single women. This book
will bring comfort and renewal for all those living with "enforced
singleness," as well as challenge all of us to show more empathy and
nurture within the real needs of Christian community today.

JAMES M. HOUSTON
*Founding principal of Regent College, Vancouver, Canada,
and professor emeritus of spiritual theology*

Revelations of a Single Woman gives an articulate, humorous,
and candid voice to so many of my same desires, struggles, and
fears as a single woman. Connally runs emotionally naked through
this book. It is so refreshing to read a book on singlehood by an
author who is (gasp) single. She sets the example of living a life
full of honest expression that is ultimately surrendered to a God
who is worthy of our complete faith and trust. Every friend, relative,
and pastor of a single woman should read *Revelations of a Single Woman*.

Do you really want to know what it's like to be living (and really trying to love) a life you didn't expect? Read this book. This is what it's like.

AMY TAYLOR
Program director, Habitat for Humanity of Greater Los Angeles

Connally Gilliam has written a remarkable, moving, and inspirational book. I have already given the book, with the strongest of recommendations, to both of my single daughters, as well as to my wife, a professional psychotherapist. Connally Gilliam is to be commended for writing a book that will make a real difference in the lives of those who read it.

DR. RICHARD LAND
President, Southern Baptist Ethics & Religious Liberty Commission and author of
Imagine! A God-Blessed America: How It Could Happen and
What It Would Look Like

What a relief to laugh and cry at the exploration of pertinent issues that society has yet to figure out how to graciously address. Connally's book serves as a great spiritual and practical compass for single women attempting to navigate the myriad of uncharted professional and social arenas now open to us. It is refreshing to read that other women in other cities are facing the same challenges, asking the same questions, and wrestling to find the same fulfillment that I am.

RACHEL KRAINES

Serious, brutally honest, and easy to read. And it keeps a sense of humor (without any silliness or fluff). This is one of those topics that is difficult to broach rationally and impossible to deal with emotionally, yet she does both perfectly. The demographic changes that are upon us are here to stay, so far as I can tell, and this is going to be a very important guide for so many.

JAMES DAVISON HUNTER
Author of Evangelicalism: The Coming Generation

I've started reading a few Christian singles books. This is the first
one I've finished. And reread. And recommended. This is not
another book on how to survive being single! It's an authentic
look at singleness—including the difficulties and disappointments—
in the context of *living*.

SARAH MASON, 23, CHICAGO

Connally Gillam tackles the subject of unintentional singleness
with something so fresh—so true—that this book feels like one long,
cool cup of water. It's full of insight and encouragement
for any woman navigating the changing landscape of
relationships, marriage, and singleness.

PAULA RINEHART
Author of Strong Women, Soft Hearts *and* Sex and the Soul of a Woman

I found it to be insightful and honest, with a refreshing dose
of humor and candor. She masterfully articulates the fact that
the issues and struggles are *real*, yet she gently leads the reader
again and again to the God of hope who can and will meet
us in our places of pain and disappointment. Gilliam dares
to discuss even the secret and seldom talked about topics that
face single women without coming across as preachy or
prudish; her openhearted style draws the reader in.
I am anxious to recommend it to my friends!

KELLI DONOVAN, 36, DENVER

The bracing and soul-strengthening work Connally Gilliam
has done in this book will be a continuing blessing to singles,
and to those everywhere who love them.

FREDERICA MATHEWES-GREEN
Author of Gender: Men, Women, Sex, and Feminism

Connally Gilliam bravely opens up to us by sharing her journey in a postmodern world, where the reasonable expectations for life, career, marriage, and family are in a continual state of change. In a delightful manner (and with a surprising lack of man bashing), she provides a welcome respite from the continuous flow of "how-to" books for singles. *Revelations of a Single Woman* is absolutely timely and provides the honesty and insight that are needed.

ELIZABETH WEBB
Actress, playwright, and filmmaker, New York

Connally Gilliam has found her voice for speaking to an entire generation of women. She has done so in a way that helps us all understand the biblical and cultural vocabulary needed for a genuinely personal approach to singleness in a post-personal era.

DR. JOSEPH "SKIP" RYAN
Senior minister, Park Cities Presbyterian Church, Dallas, and author of
That You May Believe: Studies in the Gospel of John *and*
Worship: Beholding the Beauty of the Lord

Connally's book is a collection of field notes for women living on the uncharted frontierlands of unintentional single life. The stories and experiences she catalogs here will be both laughably and painfully familiar.

LIZ KIMBERLIN
Graduate student, Philadelphia

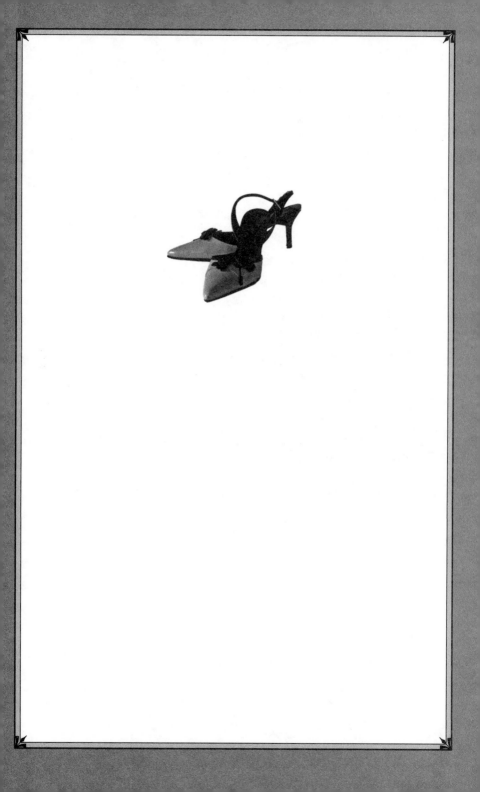

REVELATIONS

of a

Single Woman

loving the life i didn't expect

CONNALLY GILLIAM

SALT**RIVER**®

AN IMPRINT OF
TYNDALE HOUSE PUBLISHERS, INC.

Visit Tyndale's exciting Web site at www.tyndale.com

TYNDALE is a registered trademark of Tyndale House Publishers, Inc.

SaltRiver and the SaltRiver logo are registered trademarks of Tyndale House Publishers, Inc.

Revelations of a Single Woman

Library of Congress Cataloging-in-Publication Data

Gilliam, Connally.
   Revelations of a single woman : loving the life I didn't expect / Connally Gilliam.
     p. cm.

   Includes bibliographical references and index.
   ISBN-13: 978-1-4143-0308-6 (sc : alk. paper)
   ISBN-10: 1-4143-0308-4 (sc : alk. paper)
   1. Gilliam, Connally.   2. Single women—Religious life.   3. Christian women—Religious life.   I. Title.

BV4596.S5.G55 2006
248.8'432——dc22   2005017290

Printed in the United States of America

12 11 10 09 08 07 06
7 6 5 4 3 2

I dedicate this book to the many wonderful women I know
who were, are, or are yet to be single. May you know—deep down in your
"knower"—that you are the beloved of the triune God.
And may you embrace the opportunity to joyfully participate with him
in his grand purposes, now and into eternity.

I write because I want to tell something that makes me glad and strong. I want to say it, and so try to say it. Things come to me in gleams and flashes, sometimes in words themselves, and I want to weave them into a melodious, harmonious whole.

ANDREW TO ALEXA IN *The Elect Lady* BY GEORGE MACDONALD

TABLE OF CONTENTS

A Happy and Satisfying Life?

❦

"With countless options and all the freedom I'll ever need, comes the pressure to find the perfect life." So reads the subtitle of a *Newsweek* editorial by Jenny Norenberg, a woman in her mid-twenties. Citing technology and globalization, which have "brought the world to our doorstep," Norenberg writes of a generation of women who, now living between college and marriage, have been raised to believe that the world could be theirs. And now, out in that world, these women are "unsteadily navigating a barrage of choices our mothers never had the chance to make."[1] Norenberg says it well, and I couldn't agree with her more.

As a microscopic example, I think of one of my best friends since middle school, Polly. We grew up as neighbors just a block apart. She ventured off to the University of North Carolina for college; I went a few miles down the street to the University of Virginia. Since then, between the two of us we've lived or worked in seven cities on two coasts. We've landed in Seattle, DC, Philly, Vancouver, Williamsburg, Durham, and good old Charlottesville, Virginia, our hometown. As of this writing, we're both single, childless, and in our thirties. For better or for worse, neither of our lives looks much like our mothers' lives. They were both married in their early twenties and had children—Polly has one brother; I have two. Now each is still married and has lived in Charlottesville for many years—almost thirty years in my mom's case and almost forty for Polly's mother. It is a different world.

As another snapshot of change, I think simply of my career track. Whew! Its diversity and, I prefer to think, creative path could make one's head spin. First came a year of seminary after college, and then to graduate school in order to qualify for teaching high school English. From there, I served up *Romeo and Juliet* and *Julius Caesar* to teenagers until, after four years, I admitted it just wasn't for me. Off I went to work at a place called the Center for Urban and Theological Studies (affectionately known as CUTS). There I once again got to teach writing—this time to adults—and practice my rather lame administrative assistant skills for the president. "I think, sir, your flight is number 215 at 1:05. Or, oops, is that number 105 at 2:15?"

Eventually, that came to an end and led to another move—this time to be nearer to home and closer to some friends. After a short stint schlepping handbags at a very nice store where commissions on Ferragamo bags were great, I landed a job at a public policy think tank, the Center for Strategic and International Studies. While my international affairs knowledge was a little malnourished ("Um, Nicole, could you explain to me exactly what this NATO thing is?"), I did get the chance to write a few grants and learn all kinds of things about DC life. Then, finally, I found the courage to make the leap into my current profession, working for the Navigators, doing what I like to call "life coaching from a faith-based perspective" with twenty-somethings.

In short, in my own life, and in the lives of my friends and colleagues, I've seen that twenty- and thirty-something, single professional women are part of a generation that has been set free—and resourced intellectually and personally—to go and do virtually anything. What a strange, new privilege! From my travels throughout Europe, the Middle East, and Asia, and my elementary study of history, I've seen that young, educated single women in the United States are living a slice of history unlike that of almost any other place or era. And as Norenberg says, there is something "fabulous" bubbling in all this opportunity. It is the chance, she says, to freely build—without the "out" of blaming others—a "happy and satisfying life."[2]

But as I have journeyed, I've been compelled to ask some questions. Perhaps the compulsion has come from yet unmet dreams of an ideal husband, a lasting local group of friends like they have on *Friends*, or my own place decked out from the Pottery Barn. Maybe it's just my wiring. Regardless, when I pushed into my upper twenties and then my early thirties, I began running out of breath waiting for that toe-tingling husband or a perfect career to appear. I couldn't help but ask, *What exactly is a happy and satisfying life?* And as an unintentionally single woman living in an urban, transient culture, *Just how does one find or make that life?*

As I began listening to my own heart and the endless stories of a number of friends—woven into wonderings about work, men, friends, and family—I began to realize that such questions could not be answered without addressing issues that are deeper still. Perhaps you are familiar with some of those deep questions. You know . . . *Is there a God? If there is, Is he real, present, powerful, and loving?* Or in short, *Can I trust him? Even with work, men, friends, and family?* This book, then, is simply a collection of tales that reflect the story of a woman, accompanied by her widespread network of friends, in search of answers to these kinds of key life questions. So what does it take to create a happy and satisfying life? And where is God in the midst of it all?

When I was working at CUTS, a few jobs back, I had the privilege of teaching a composition course entitled *Finding Our Voice; Writing Our Story.* It was designed to develop basic writing skills in adult students while simultaneously helping them trace the finger of God in their own lives. You might be able to imagine the content: journaling, reading, reflective essays—all kinds of things to help folks live a self-examined life, then get it down in words. After endless assignments, the semester culminated with the "I Am" paper, a mini-autobiography of sorts, to be read aloud.

I will never forget the last class of the semester when Sherry, a fifty-year-old African-American woman, stood up and boldly read her "I Am" paper. She spoke as a woman who for most of her life had not believed she had a story, at least not one that mattered. But she spoke now with a depth of conviction that came from the center of her heart. The class seemed to sense this. They listened as her once quiet voice grew bold. As she recounted tales of her raw childhood, a teen marriage, and years since working jobs and raising children, the class grew silent, as if in awe. Until the end. Then the students erupted in praise, responding wholeheartedly to both the vulnerability and the truth they'd heard.

In later reflection, I realized that the power of that evening had been unleashed in part because those students had courageously looked at their own lives and labored to find words for their stories. Their lives contained, on the whole, much suffering. Poverty, abandonment, divorce, oppression, self-hatred, and abuse riddled their stories. It was no surprise that folks wanted to avoid looking too closely, let alone putting their stories onto paper. But as they took the risk of going there, and of looking carefully for God's finger—including moments when the trail went cold—what emerged were stories of survival, provision, triumph over adversity, success, reunion, and joy. And as these students slowly discovered, their seemingly small stories were woven into a much bigger drama, which included a good God who was decidedly at work. Perhaps life was hard, and these students were not always happy, but even a random stranger popping into class could have sensed the satisfaction in the room.

In many ways, my story pales in comparison to the stories of some of these men and women, though perhaps that's really what we each think about our own tale. Nevertheless, this is my honest attempt to "go there." Just like I asked my students to do, I've sought to go there around the real-life issues (mine and others') of singleness, sexuality, relationships, work, community, family, and assorted odds and ends. And also like my students, I have traced the finger of God in my life and the lives of my friends. It is not an uninterrupted straight line. It meanders through tough, tender, and faintly ridiculous territory. But I've been encouraged by so much of what I have discovered, not the least of which is that, like my students, my life is part of a bigger, God-shaped drama.

Hopefully, ideally, prayerfully, I've written these stories and reflections with enough candor that they can serve as an encouragement to my friends and readers. If I've done my job, somewhere in the pages of this book is something of the kind of inspiration that I found in that CUTS classroom. I so want people—I'm thinking now of my twenty- and thirty-something girlfriends—to discover the real source of what is fabulous. I yearn for my friends to know where life is truly found, even in a crazy culture where many of us, between sips of latte, text messages, and blind dates, scratch our heads and try to understand. Of course, I know I have friends, and perhaps a few readers, who might not believe what I say about God. I know many folks who might find my talk of a triune God—a Father, Son, and Holy Spirit— slightly outmoded or too absolute. I hate that thought because I so love my friends and yearn for us to be at home, together, in matters of truth and faith. But it's a risk I have to take in order to tell the story "true from start to finish."[3]

So, anyhow, that's what I hope to do: reflect in little snatches a larger story that meets the reader, meets *you*, at points where you really live. For instance, have you ever just laughed out loud, so long and hard that your eyes began to water? Like when you and your friend both spot that mightily endowed woman in the flowered muumuu, prancing with her poodle down the street—and you both start cracking up uncontrollably? Or have you ever felt so sad that you just curled up into the fetal position, pulled the down comforter over your head, and cried? Perhaps it happened when closure with that man—the one you thought might really have been the one—became undeniably, finally final? Hopefully, something in this string of tales will make sense to you in that place that laughs and in that place that cries.

If you're single, female, and living the life you didn't expect—or none of the above—maybe after you read, you'll know more of the Other and the others who are really with you in this journey. And who knows, perhaps something will cause you to consider new things about what constitutes a truly happy and a satisfying life. Or, if that's a bit too much to ask, maybe you'll simply put the book down and mutter to yourself, "Hmmm . . . that wasn't too bad, not too bad at all."

CHAPTER 1

An Uncharted Desert Isle

Over the years, a number of friends have shared with me that the best thing they have ever done was to jettison the crazy dysfunctions or strangling grip of the generations before them. Shaking the dust off their feet from legacies of abuse or addiction has been a privilege. The past, more than one friend has said, needs to be left behind. But while I have related to this in part—I'd love to be fully free of the racism tainting my Southern heritage or the devaluing of "feminine" traits such as mystery or intuition implicit within my Protestant background—there are certain aspects of my past that I have always longed to hold on to. Modify, perhaps, but hold on to nevertheless.

I think of my mom, who was married in her early twenties and had three children. She's the daughter of a woman who married in her early twenties and had three children. And *she* was the daughter of a woman who married in her early twenties and had two. An assumed paradigm shaped my mother's, grandmother's, and great-grand-mother's lives. It centered around some givens—like loving God and people; marrying young, having babies, and building families; laughing in the always-busy kitchen; and inviting others in. There is a core legacy of vegetable gardens, rolled-up sleeves, hot soup, and blanket shaking. These women's lives were not limited to those givens by any stretch—all three went to college, ran organizations, and, in my mother's case, served on boards, but the givens were the building blocks on which life was constructed. I have not wanted to let those givens go. I always figured that twenty-five might be a nice age for marriage.

Of course, I've never hankered to morph into June Cleaver from *Leave It to Beaver*—after all, I like to wear jeans, and my vision has always outstripped domestic duties. But June Cleaver was never these matriarchs' reality, and she's not what I'm talking about. I'm talking about a framework that, in my experience, created space for good, if decidedly imperfect, things to happen. Good things like forming communities of messy families which, headed by one man and one woman imperfectly loving one another, in turn created space for imperfect kids to live, explore, fail, and dream.

The reality is, however, that these and many more experiences as givens have been leaking out of the broader culture for a long time. Their slow exit has left my guts in a low-grade cringe for a while. Like a child straddling the center of a seesaw, I've teetered between that solid world of givens and the increasing counterweight of other worlds over the years.

There was the early lesson learned when Mr. Nixon's cronies (including my good friend's dad) went to jail for Watergate—*can't trust the president.* There were beloved and trusted high school teachers who promoted their confident agnosticism—*teachers don't always have all the answers.* Or a dear college friend who, after falling in love and getting pregnant, endured a wrenching abortion while I made vain, nineteen-year-old attempts to walk with her—*life isn't always easy.* There were those two neighborhood girls who each married young (in their early twenties), but then each divorced before the dust had settled—*the "marry young" thing doesn't always work.* Add to that a few experiences with men who were keen to get to know me until it cost them some personal convenience—*guys, who are supposed to "lead," aren't all dying for the marriage dance.*

Throw on top of that the confusion about a profession—Just what is this whole career thing supposed to be about anyway? Is it always progress to move up the ladder? And how do you know?—and the list could go on and on. Whatever gaps in this life have remained have been steadily filled by the relentless onslaught of change agents: microwaves, e-mail, shifting national demographics, and economic globalization. You get the picture.

My mother said once in a moment of candor, "I feel as if I've enriched you for a world that no longer trades in our currency." A treasure chest of Confederate cash, you might say. She was, at least in part, right. While I still know how to grow tomatoes and make vegetable soup from scratch—and do—the wildly shifting culture has a gravitational pull that I've not been able to control. The seesaw has tilted, and the bottom line is that, try as I might, I haven't been able to find my way back home, at least to the home of my mothers. The past really is the past. As much as I've wanted to deny it, and as hard as I've worked to change it (find that man, simplify my life, build a world where I know how to operate), I am in my upper thirties, single, making my own money (of sorts), and foiled in almost every attempt to birth some past paradigm into my present life. My life is now sprinkled with—or, more honestly, *shaped by*—irrepressible technology, speed, and change. That's reality.

I hate this because sometimes I feel scared. It's like looking over my shoulder and noticing that the bridge leading back home has collapsed. That sinking feeling in my gut returns. The theme song from

Gilligan's Island pops into my mind: "The ship struck ground on the shores of this uncharted desert isle, with Gilligan, the skipper too, the millionaire and his wife . . ." An uncharted desert isle: that's where I have landed.

Growing up, I read (at least four times) the Laura Ingalls Wilder *Little House on the Prairie* series. I thought nothing could be more fun than to be a pioneer with a big, strong "Manly look-alike" husband. It seemed as if a pioneer life would stretch me in its simple, if relentless, rigor and that somehow fighting out hard winters with others—milking the cow in a blizzard, making snow ice cream, etc.—would satisfy me deeply. However, I never dreamed that the uncharted desert island in which I would "pioneer" would be in Washington, DC, and that I'd first have to learn how to find a skipper, a millionaire, and the rest amid hundreds of thousands of people. But here I am.

I think of a greeting card I once received. The cover pictured a windblown cow sporting sunglasses against the backdrop of whirling neon lights. The caption read, "Dorothy, you're not in Kansas anymore." It cracked me up even as I cringed. "But I liked Kansas! If this is Oz, send me home."

The truth is, however, that although there might be no place like home, there are also no sparkly red shoes to get me back there. I have clicked my heels and mantra-ed until I'm blue in the face, but I'm still stuck in a world replete with wicked witches, fake wizards, and a bunch of kindhearted munchkins (not to mention a few other traveling companions). It feels a lot like an uncharted desert isle where all I have left is an internal imprint, one that shaped my expectations for life but doesn't fit easily into the world I have been catapulted into.

So what do I do? If in my heart of hearts, after the adrenaline of being marooned on the uncharted desert isle dies down, I really do miss Kansas—or more accurately, the best parts of Tyler, Texas, or Charlottesville, Virginia—what do I do? The "doer" in me determines to dream up alternative realities: a commune in the Virginia foothills, an urban enclave with diverse neighbors, front porches, and corner stores . . . the whole village raising the children . . . perhaps going on a special mission to a foreign land, with a team who would function "all for one and one for all." However, my few attempts in these directions have not worked; it's easier to dream than to create. So my temptation, as you might imagine, is finally to sit on the stairs of my rented house and cry. Or, when I'm in an ornery mood, circle the wagons and try to hold off the outside world.

Problem is, I can't do either of these things for long. Eventually, one has to get up off the stairs to go eat. And meanwhile, living in an age of global everything, it's virtually impossible to create an insular world. However, even if I could overcome these obstacles and hide, one big barrier remains: I can't escape the real presence of a God who continues to call me to love him and to love others, regardless of where I find myself.

My mom, in her humility, was basically right. The culture of my past has bequeathed me a chest full of currency, much of it now undervalued; I know rules for games that almost nobody plays anymore. Rightly or wrongly, salad fork placement isn't so crucial in a fast food world. But one piece of my past that is galvanized in my soul, one thing that neither seesaws, nor wrecked boats, nor new territories seem able to knock out of me, is the reality of words I heard my mother and her mother (and perhaps her mother too) say: "Just remember, only two things are eternal: God (and his Word), and the souls of people."

It sounds so simplistic, so quaintly anachronistic. And the English major in me has asked questions over the years like: What does it mean that something is *eternal?* What is the *Word of God?* And please, who really can define the *soul* of a person? But even as I've asked, I've not been able to escape the reality behind those words. Like a compass, those words have pointed me to a God who is still real, even after dreams have failed to materialize. They have pointed me to bigger truths, even when my little life looks like nothing I ever anticipated. They have served as "true north" for me: what matters is God and people.

Honestly, I'm very glad that there is something that lasts, something that is real, something that matters. In college I decided that if Kafka was right and we are in essence cockroaches (my very lay interpretation of his philosophy), then I'd accept that. But amazingly, in spite of the roller coaster of change and so many givens having been flung into space, I somehow continue to "know in my knower"—as an elderly African-American woman I once met called gut-level conviction—that God and people really *are*. These building blocks are eternal.

Frameworks about when and whom and how to marry might be up for grabs; confusion over the nature of work might continue; debates about the essentials—or lack thereof—of gender might rage; and a myriad of other wild cards might get thrown onto the table, but really, none of that ultimately matters. As important as these questions are, the answers to them do not, at root, define me. Sure, I've always hoped that my life might be a Broadway musical, with big choruses singing and dancing while Mr. Right and I twirl into oblivion. But in an unanticipated way, the chaos of the culture in which I now find myself twirling is becoming for me a strange, unsolicited gift with far greater depth than Rodgers and Hammerstein could have ever foreseen.

In large part, the gift has taken the form of a push. Living in a world I cannot even pretend to control, whose rules prove consistently elusive, I've been pushed toward creative dependence on God and other people. I carry in my mind an image of the westward move of the railroad across the United States: I see sweaty people riding on one of those flat train cars propelled by their own effort. (Can you picture the team of people pumping the handle back and forth?) In contrast, I've wanted to run on an inherited grooved track, flying smoothly like a high-speed train into the horizon. And I have spent endless hours of analysis, angst, and tears trying to bring this about. But instead, what's really been happening is that I—with the much-needed help of so many others—have simply been slowly moving forward, laying one section of track at a time, praying that wild animals won't eat any of us along the way.

Lest the picture be too one-sided, however, I have gotten wonderful tastes of life en route—moments when, gathered around that homemade soup, laughter infects a table full of friends; times when I see a group I'm leading coalesce around a burgeoning vision; or instances when, driving in the car, I gaze out the window at the ever-dancing sky and feel in awe of the loving people God has woven into my life. These tastes are delicious. They are perhaps doubly sweet because they often emerge out of what can seem like the lifeless ashes of a busy, cynical, and detached age.

I'm starting to suspect that the craziness of our current culture and the loss of so many givens might be proving, at least in my life, to be the thing that Sheldon Vanauken referenced in his book *A Severe Mercy*. His wife's early death was the push that catapulted him into a far greater understanding of the love they had shared and of the God who had made that love possible. Though he grieved her passing, he could not deny the gifts that came with it. For me, the craziness and loss have shaken me so hard that though my teeth haven't fallen out (yet), my tight grip on the good things from the past, real or imagined, has been loosened. My hands are more open to receive whatever gifts God wants to give me in the present.

The Old Testament patriarch Abraham was commended by a New Testament writer for his willingness to keep going even when the path was not clear. "By faith," the author of the book of Hebrews wrote, "Abraham, when called to go to a place he would later receive as his inheritance, obeyed and went, *even though he did not know where he was going.*"[4] Virtually clueless about where this journey would take him, by *faith*—by knowing in his knower what is real and eternal—he kept going, wandering through much desert on his journey.

Perhaps Abraham got scared and burst into tears along the way. Or perhaps as the adrenaline of the journey wore off he dreamed of going back to the days when he was named Abram and lived in good old Ur of the Chaldeans, as his neck of the woods was called. Maybe not; I might just be imposing my own psychological profile on the man. But regardless, like Abraham, I want to keep going by faith. For better or for worse, my life does not look much like those of my foremothers. But regardless, I gratefully take with me the inherited and life-giving knowledge that God and people matter. In the end, these are the best building blocks I could have. These truths are the rails on which I sweat, rest, and am learning to run.

CHAPTER 2

The Dork

In addition to displaying drawings by her young Picassoesque grand-children, my mother's refrigerator is home to an endless array of cartoons, some as old as twenty years. The cartoons reflect my mom's values and sense of humor. Some are self-deprecating—mocking, for instance, my mother's longtime love affair with health foods. Others are tongue-in-cheek social commentary. But there's one that has always cracked me up. A lone, silly-looking man sits on a stool in his kitchen, party hat on, blower in hand, with a big banner behind him. The caption reads: "Horace Snodgrass celebrates his 20th homeschool reunion!" That idea just makes me chuckle. A homeschool reunion of one. Poor Horace. I look at the cartoon, shaking my head and thinking with a low-level, cartoon-grade compassion, *Ah, the epitome of "The Dork."*

On New Year's Eve, at the age of thirty-six and still highly chagrined that I was about to be thirty-seven and could no longer call myself "early thirties" (a descriptor I felt I could reasonably use until that point), I headed back to DC from a Christmas spent with my family in central Virginia. Much to my delight, I'd had three invitations to New Year's Eve events and had finally decided on a dinner party with a group of former colleagues, now friends. That way I would avoid the smoke-laden chaos of the mass, parking-challenged, downtown party, while also sidestepping the group of quiet, serious reflectors who would want to recount their thematic discoveries of the past year (I do that a lot naturally and wasn't in the mood for it on a holiday). Pleased with my decision, I e-mailed the host couple, Ron and Kirsten, and said, "Love to come. What can I bring?" Ron suggested that I help out with the beverages and told me that he was expecting eleven to thirteen people. He reminded me not to wear black (their dog had a shedding problem) and said how glad he was that I was coming.

I stopped by the grocery to grab drinks and went on my way. Dressed in my nonblack clothes, I arrived a little late and joined the already lively conversation. I was innocently nibbling my mini-quiches and baby carrots when it began to dawn on me that I was the only person at the party not attached to another. Suddenly I found myself wishing for that group of quiet, serious reflectors with whom I could share all my deep insights! I'd been so busy during the Christmas hubbub that I hadn't focused on Ron's comments. If I had, I might have realized that both eleven and thirteen are odd numbers, which, if divided by two—the number in a couple—leaves a remainder. In an adrenaline-induced flash, a rather painfully electric insight coursed through my entire nervous system: "YOU, Connally, ARE THE REMAINDER!"

Faced with this most nauseating realization, I figured it was time for a regrouping trip to the restroom. In my little silent cell, I managed to assess the situation. *Hey, here I am. I'm okay. I'm not a loser. I like these peo-*

ple. I'm confident in myself. Plus, maybe God wants to love people through me or something! Right, God? It's not supposed to be all about me? Right? It's about caring for others? Right? Can't say that I really heard anything in response, but a few minutes later I emerged, lipstick redone, ready to go. I marched back in, filled up my plate, got a drink, and began conversing here and there, picking stray dog hairs off my sweater, and periodically reminding myself, *Remember, girl, you had three invitations!*

For a few blissful hours, I lost track of the numbers and enjoyed just being with my friends as midnight approached. With about five minutes to go before the ball was to drop and Dick Clark would do his thing, Ron passed out blowers and confetti and poppers of all descriptions. Standing up together, we all counted down . . . five . . . four . . . three . . . two . . . one. "Happy New Year!" we all shouted at the top of our lungs. "Happy New Year!" And then it happened. One of a single woman's top ten nightmares. I was standing there alone, with my pointy party hat and blower, while every person around me magnetically embraced his or her significant other. I was floating alone in a sea of long, celebratory, impassioned, wet kisses.

On *Baywatch*, when all the beautiful, well-sculpted California lifeguards are called down the beach for a rescue, the action is always filmed in slow motion: Barbie- and Ken-like bodies languidly leaping and bouncing along like hypnotized fairies. In the same way, in Ron and Kirsten's living room, Dick Clark's flickering image suddenly seemed to fade far away and the in-house action seemed to last ten times its normal duration. Standing there alone, trying to look perfectly natural and positively delighted to be blowing my blower—repeatedly—there crept over me the frightful feeling of kinship with dear Horace Snodgrass from the fridge. I thought to myself, "Connally, you are a dork!"

Eventually, perhaps out of pity or plain friendliness, Ron broke what I'll call the suspended animation of the moment ("magic" just doesn't have quite the right connotation). He stopped kissing his wife and kissed me on the cheek. "Happy New Year, Con." I managed to reply, "Oh, uh, yeah, Happy New Year, Ron!"

Single girlfriends and I have laughed until we've cried revisiting that story. And my dad, in spite of his well-trained attempts to be sensitive to his emotionally high-maintenance daughter, about fell out of his chair when I shared it with him. Honestly, the laughter alone has almost redeemed the experience. But something else has been born from that story of single social "mistfitness" and ones like it: I have learned a greater degree of empathy than I ever would have hoped. I have learned what it is to be the odd one out.

Growing up, though I often *felt* left out, I never particularly *looked* left out to others. Okay, I didn't get on the homecoming court in high school, and I didn't win "Best All Around" in the senior superlatives (not that I'm bitter), but on the whole, I did okay. With the help of two best friends, I somehow found a third way between the super-popular, cool, party kids and the smart, nice, do-the-right-thing kids. As a result, for the most part, I was not the last person picked for the kickball team, so to speak, and even managed to be a captain occasionally. But in this whole mating game, I was—and am still—standing by the fence, waiting, my singleness evident.

Of course, the way I'm talking, it sounds like singleness is some horrible disease. It is not a disease. A few weeks spent in India showed me people with real diseases. Even closer to home, I have friends who have carried with them both physical pain and emotional wounds that they cannot laugh about. So I want to keep the Horace/singleness analogy in its right place. Having said that, however, there is something about being unintentionally single that can leave one feeling "dis-eased" in a couples' world.

In the hysterically funny, if profane, book *Bridget Jones's Diary*, Bridget, the single, thirty-something protagonist, finds herself seated at a dinner table with all couples. "Bridge," asks the female half of one couple, "why are there so many single girls in their thirties?" With a feigned innocence, Bridget cheekily replies, "I don't know. . . . Perhaps it's because beneath our clothes we have scales all over our bodies?" It is a funny line, matched only by the humor of the couples who awkwardly attempt to respond. But it's also a memorable line. Almost every single woman I know who saw the movie remembers it. It matches felt experience "spot on," as Bridget would say.

While home with me for a Thanksgiving holiday (during which I'd been thinking, *I should be here with a husband and kids, not friends*), a friend of mine said that "no offense," but she was glad I was single. Not knowing exactly how to respond, I paused, then asked, "Uh . . . why?" She went on to explain that my being single didn't make sense to her. In her analysis, there were no major family issues. No residual hatred of men that she could observe. No big, hairy warts on my nose. In short, she couldn't see the reason. And that was a comfort to her. *Strange reasoning*, I thought. For her, however, it was a small reminder that, contrary to what she was always tempted to believe, unmet desires are not necessarily divine punishment for a flaw. Sometimes, when we line it all up, life simply is not fair.

More important, my friend continued, my unintended singleness made me more approachable, more human. As she experienced it, my disappointment was a chink in the armor of my personality that let more of my heart out and gave others something softer to grab on to.

Frankly, I didn't really want to hear that. My heart was already soft enough, and even if it wasn't, I still think I could come up with roughly 153 alternative means for accomplishing this same heart-changing end. But that Thanksgiving conversation has stayed with me. I knew, and still know, that she was right. My unintended singleness, in addition to giving me some humorous stories that help me entertain or bond with a willing audience, undeniably has changed the contours of my heart. In bringing me into all-too-tender touch with my inner (and outer) dork, for lack of a better term, I've grown kinder, and I'm glad for the change.

I think back to that cartoon of homeschooled Horace. It still makes me chuckle. I wish you could see it. But I think what's funny, too, is that the quality of my chuckle has changed over the years. (The cartoon has been on the fridge for a long time!) Had I laughed at Horace or a flesh-and-blood counterpart twenty years ago, my guffaws might have carried with them a fearful undercurrent of, "Oh, Lord, let me never be a social reject like Horace!" But this crazy singleness thing with its collection of "standing with the blower, alone at the party" experiences has changed a lot of that in me. I think that if Horace wandered onto our field after school now, I'd be far kinder to him than I would have been twenty years ago. I might even be able to give him an empathetic grin and ask him to play on my kickball team.

CHAPTER 3

Our Many Selves

For two days I sit in a cross-cultural ministry seminar at a place called the Hope Center in southeast DC. Around me are folks who live among the urban poor for the sake of incarnating their faith in Jesus. As I sit here listening, a large part of my heart is brought to life. I listen to stories of interactions with drug addicts and almost-parentless kids; I listen to discussions of racial and cultural differences and the struggles such differences incite. I am reminded of my two years in Philly, when I had the rare experience (for a white person) of working and living in a neighborhood as a minority. While the amazing architecture surrounding me was crumbling, I had the privilege of interacting with people whose hearts and lives were being rebuilt, even soaring. Sitting now in these meetings I can't help but wonder, *Is this me? Should I be back in this urban ministry world full-time?*

Snapping me out of my musings, the seminar ends. I hop into my car, drive twelve minutes, and walk into my brick Virginia home. I've forgotten, but the home owner, my housemate Dolly, is hosting her National Cotillion Debutante Sponsors group cocktail party. Within moments, in my jeans and sweater, I find myself whisked into a world of brilliant hors d'oeuvres, men in silk ties, and a conversation with Studie, the grande dame of the cotillion, a diminutive eighty-year-old blonde gal whose wit always brings me up short and leaves me smiling. I make small talk for a minute discussing horse farms, summer camps, and Virginia colleges. It is easy conversation, culturally familiar, and I float through it popping ham biscuits into my mouth. Then, excusing myself as horribly underdressed, I sneak downstairs to my basement room to change and chill a bit before deciding whether or not to return.

No sooner have I changed, however, than my other housemate and her brand-new boyfriend come down the stairs. They almost tumble down—reminiscent of two high schoolers happily escaping their parents. A mutual friend had introduced them, and the Internet had been their go-between. Now Greg has flown three thousand miles from an island off the coast of Washington state to meet Kate in person.

Noticing my roommate's mesmerized and love-struck gaze, I check him out. Handsome dude. Tan, angular, facial-haired, Birkenstock-clad, pierced ear (hole, no ring)—decidedly Northwestern-looking. As the three of us talk about boats and salmon and breaching whales, I think, *Now here is a down-to-earth guy. Wish more people in DC were like this.* Suddenly I'm wondering if perhaps I should be living a life of bread baking, composting, and 6 a.m. hikes.

Eventually I excuse myself and this time head for the bathroom to renew my lipstick. (Would I wear lipstick if I were living off home-made goat cheese?) Looking in the mirror, I exhale. Staring back at me is a Picassoesque portrait: multiple, fragmented facets of the same face. I am reminded of his famous painting *Girl Before a Mirror*. In my case, I see who I've been in the last three hours: urban ministry devotee, debutante, and outdoorsy granola chick. I want to beg, "Will the real self please stand up?"

Have you ever had that sensation? Have you ever felt as if you were many selves—and each is you but none of them is fully you? And have you ever yearned for those many parts to come together somehow, somewhere, with someone? My friend Steph says that fragmentation is part of her compulsion to find a husband quickly. She writes,

> I guess [because there is no quick fix to fragmentation] that I go back to desiring someone (specifically a mate) who puts certain parameters on my life, just by way of being a defining area of my life that keeps me from disjointing so much. But if my outward fragmentation is simply an outpouring of the fragmentation within, then that relationship will never accomplish this—certainly not as its sole use.

Feeling scattered is not a new experience for women, married or single. Women's lives are often talked about in "seasons" or "chapters," and women's identities are often defined in relational (and therefore multiple) terms—wife, mother, sister, daughter, friend, neighbor, colleague, and so forth. But Steph is picking up on how living single in a world replete with options—free of the familial ties that tend to bind—seems to compound this sense of fragmentation.

The splintering process works in and on us in two ways. The first way (and I'm not sure which is the chicken and which is the egg; perhaps it's simply a tag team affair) is obvious. Most if not all of us come out of childhood—or maybe even out of the womb—with a variety of traits, gifts, aspirations, and desires, a number of which contradict one another. I have one friend who nearly pulled her hair out over the question, *Am I more "country club" or "alternative music scene"?* She flipped back and forth for a while, but in the end she saw that she was both.

Likewise, how many times have I heard my not single, not twenty- or thirty-something mother sigh, "Oh, if only I had about a dozen more lives. There are so many things I'd still love to do" (like be a therapist, go on an archaeological dig, see a few more good operas, and spend a summer at the beach with a box of all the books she's yet to read, to name a few). Cats seem to get it right with nine lives!

What is unique, however, is the other splinterer: our context. Now all of us have seemingly endless opportunities to live out our varied and often conflicting selves. For example, we now have the option to cross cultures like never before. Let's face it, thirty years ago your average white girl from my Virginia neighborhood would not have been moving to inner-city Philly to work and live. And with the Internet we have the option to connect with people who live three thousand miles away, all with a few clicks on the screen. We can always find those who share a similar background with us, while still maintaining the option to move on. Life doesn't demand those historic or familial links. Just think of the slew of women single-handedly buying and selling their own cute homes, far from families. That's a new phenomenon. We might not be able to have it all, but that's only because our arms aren't big enough to hold the swirling morass; most of it is now decidedly up for grabs.

Maybe this splintering wouldn't be problematic if the people around us were a constant. It would be one thing if you were the only one spinning around, expressing facets of yourself while the social structures stayed the same. But it's you and me and a whole bunch of other people. Actually, the very social structures we latch on to as we spin seem to be rife with other spinners. This is most clearly felt in young adult singles' networks.

The pattern goes something like this: You live in a city for a while and make a group of friends, normally a group of peers from the workplace, a church or synagogue, or perhaps a network of college alums. After a few years, however, those friends slowly begin to marry off, move away, or busily spin into other circles. Unlike the TV show, friends don't always stay around for ten seasons. But because they matter to you nevertheless, you remain committed to some of the scattered ones via e-mail and cell phone. Still, you need to make some new friends to fill the gaps, though this time perhaps you have a little less energy to pour out. Inevitably, however, they too marry off, move away (or you do), or busily spin into other circles. Again, you stay tangentially connected to a few. But Saturday nights continue to roll around with daunting frequency, and if you don't want to watch *Nick at Nite* reruns alone, the process continues. After a while you can start to feel as if various parts of you are poured out into many people and places—some real, some virtual, none satisfyingly constant. My friend Tracy compares it to attempting to slake one's relational thirst by sipping from a thousand little waxy Dixie cups. You don't die of dehydration, but in your core, you increasingly long for a few deep wells.

Now this might sound simply like the problem of an extrovert. And obviously personality plays into it. But it's not just a "gregarious person's" issue. One introverted friend of mine moved from a smaller city where she was finishing a graduate degree to start a new, big-responsibility government job in DC. She is a woman who likes to have just a few key friends. What she has found, however, is that even though there are six or eight times more young adults in this area, connecting with people is tougher; everyone, including her fellow introverts, is too busy embracing the options. She laughingly says that it seems like for every two or three calls she used to make in order to connect with a friend for the weekend, she now makes about six or seven. That means that if she doesn't want to watch *Nick at Nite* alone, she needs to be connected to (or scattered among) more people. That exhausts her.

So what's a woman to do? You're a fragmented girl living in a fragmented world, and you're starting to take on a scary resemblance to the girl before the mirror in Picasso's painting. Yes, the picture is colorful and interesting to study, but honestly, it's not what most of us want to look or feel like.

Recently I asked some friends for help with this question. I was feeling the effects of expanding into new realms, contracting and locking onto some relationships more deeply while having to let others go. I felt like a rock that, as a result of the capricious environment, was starting to crack and fragment on the inside. So I cried out, "Help!"

My friends are awesome. I wish, of course, that the three I am thinking of at this moment didn't live in Baltimore, Phoenix, and Albuquerque. In my fantasy life all my favorite people from throughout the world would live near each other in one large, happy community. I want a sort of comfortable and convenient "one-stop shopping" experience, as my friend Cindi calls it—some big relational Target or Wal-Mart designed for easy access. But as each of these friends reminded me in her own way, that's fantasy. Speaking independently of one another, but even speaking as married women with children, they were unanimous: *You're going to have to find a way to live in the fragmented chaos, because it's not going away anytime soon. This is the dominating reality in our generation.* They are right.

So I cried. I can prattle blithely about splintering and fragmentation, but it really does have an emotional cost, leaving one—this one, at least—feeling isolated and lonely. So I cried some more. I got on my knees and asked—yet again—*Lord, help me.* Then I flipped open my New Testament to the story of the Prodigal Son. One of these three friends had suggested I read it—she thought it might connect with the question of wholeness.

If you've not read the story, I'd recommend it to you.[5] In short, it's a story of two brothers. One stayed on his dad's estate doing his duties but with a bad attitude. The other snatched up his inheritance, lived a profligate life, and came home on his knees begging for a job so he could eat. But as I read that story, I realized that as interesting a study in diverse personalities as it is, what it's really about is the father's love for his boys—both his goody-goody and his no-good, broken boy. It's crazy. It's the father who wants connection with and restoration for his boys. It's the father who, "filled with compassion," runs out to wrap his arms around the bad boy before he can even get his "hire me" speech together. It's the father who throws this renegade a welcome-home party to beat all parties. And when the older brother starts in with the, "Whoa, this is seriously not fair—I've been here playing by the rules the whole time" shtick, it's the father who gently reminds him, "You are always with me, and everything I have is yours." In short, it's the father who yearns to see each boy whole and woven together into the family and community.

It's the Father. It's the Father. It's the Father. As I reflected on that story, I slowly began to realize, *It's the FATHER, stupid.* And then it dawned on me—the Father knows that I'm part urban ministry worker, part debutante, and part granola chick, and that a lot of those parts—plus others—don't fit together. The Father knows that good friends move away. The Father knows that family-free living can leave one too free an agent. The Father knows that committed communities fracture. The Father knows that the people around me are spinning in their crazy circles too. The Father knows that I'm drinking out of too many Dixie cups. The Father knows. But more than just knowing, he cares. That's the wild part. He has compassion. He's the one who runs out with a profoundly welcoming heart. He's the one who gently reminds me of his presence and generosity. It leaves me speechless. Or wanting to cry. Or maybe to sing.

Yesterday I read an e-mail from a consultant in Shanghai who wrote about "the floating population mentality" he has encountered in megacities. The mentality of people uprooted from tradition and in constant transition, he says, ultimately expresses itself in a chronic attitude of "I'll come *if I can*, and I'll get *what I want.*" But these people aren't just in megacities like Shanghai. They are in DC and Dallas and Denver and Detroit and many, many other places. Maybe because people scatter and relational options seem endless, we can also be tempted to treat one another as if we are in fact available for purchase (or disposal) from the nearby Mega-Mart. Then that can really mess us up!

So I have to wonder, *How does the Father's desire for his children's wholeness connect with the world of scattered friends and fragmented lives in which so many of us live?*

I think the link is this—the father-heart of God will lead us through the chaos; we simply need to grow in trust that he wants to and is capable. Cindi puts it this way:

> Sure, having your eggs in different baskets can leave you feeling fragmented because it seems to go against this thing in us that desires to go to one well, one basket, one person, one church, one department store, one whatever. But maybe this has something to do with our bent toward mindless routine. We love that. I don't have to think as much. I don't have to trust as much. It's a formula that works. Autopilot.
>
> But when I've let go of my one-stop shopping need, when I've explored other options and made myself available for provision of God's choosing, I end up more satisfied. He amazes me with his creativity and his perfect timing and his wisdom in portion control. He does more than just meet my need; he leaves me peaceful and satisfied.

Of course, now would be a great time for a compelling story that shows how the split parts of me—all the little, conflicted "Mini Me's"—have, as a result of this letting go, come home, reconciled as one. I'd love for you to see how in laying my bitter too-good and busted no-good parts before God, and growing in trust of him, I've been catapulted down a straight path of transformation. Picasso's fragmented damsel is transfigured into a vision of lovely, life-giving wholeness, complete with healthy networks and well-defined communities.

But I can't tell you this with any integrity. My cry for help in my own fragmentation was just seventeen days ago. And I've been at this trusting thing for much longer than that; clearly my path hasn't become a smooth interstate.

Still, I'm convinced that a growing trust of God's good-heartedness is the way forward. I definitely have seen changes in my friends' and my lives as we've stopped trying to make it all work and trusted God instead—changes like a greater heart rest, a deeper appreciation of others, and an increased joy in serving. But I'm also banking on the hope that if I could see the big picture, I'd see the little zigzags amid the spinning chaos as part of a much straighter path, slowly funneling us straight on toward eternity. And in eternity, there's going to be a big celebration for all of us humbled renegades and sticks-in-the-mud. Finally, a cohesive community party!

Still, I don't think trusting leads only to postmortem wholeness. I'm beginning to suspect that this culture that neurotically spins our already fragmented parts into so many places doesn't hold the final card in this life either. Sure, it can deal up loneliness and isolation. But we don't have to be scared by a world that's too fast or too complex to control, because ultimate control isn't up to us. God is big and brilliant enough to trump even the fragmentation by using the fragmentation itself to help make our paths straight. Let me give a final example.

When I lived in inner-city Philadelphia, I saw lives being transformed. But that cross-cultural voyage—head-spinning for a wide-eyed girl like me—also served to prepare me for the even crazier cultural and relational shifts I was yet to encounter. When I was working at CUTS, an urban college, I spoke with a student late one evening after class. This woman was large, vibrant, coffee-colored, and seemingly fearless. She was married, raising four kids, working as a secretary, running a food bank at her church, serving on her church's worship team, and going to college for a degree in urban ministry management. As I listened to her, I was awestruck by how she was surviving life in so many roles, with so many demands—some in the present, some still lingering from the past. "Wow," I whispered, "to be doing all this stuff you must really believe God is real."

She suddenly rolled her eyes, and then she frowned, like perhaps she'd misheard. "*Believe* God is real? Honey, I *know* God is real. Without Jesus, I'd be dead. How else could I keep going?" She was serious. She had no illusions of self-sufficiency. Her personal struggles, the chaos of her neighborhood, the seductive pulls on her kids, the poverty around her, and the challenges of living as a black woman in a world she could not control wouldn't allow such a privilege.

I did not know it at the time, but our conversation was giving me more than just a slice of multicultural pie from Mega-Mart's bakery. Her still-reverberating words were the perfect gift for me, lodging somewhere deeper than any of my urban, debutante, or granola-chick selves. Looking back I can see that at that moment, even as I was doing the very thing that has left me and so many others in a swirl—moving outside of tradition, stepping into new opportunities—the Father was already compassionately running out to meet me. Through this woman's profound and penetrating faith, he was giving me a gift he knew I would need later on down the road. The Father was priming the well in my soul with deep truth. And in so doing, he was providing for future thirsty days.

No, I've not yet stepped into nirvana. I keep yearning for the party with all the people I love. I long to be made whole. I ache for a husband to journey with. And without a doubt, just managing (let alone consolidating) a good number of the Dixie cups is tough, if not impossible, work. But as I'm seemingly zigzagging through life, my real self is slowly discovering this: Even this fragmented journey can't dry up the well because, as a woman once seared deeply into my soul, honey, I *know* God is real.

CHAPTER 4

Garden of the Heart

Miss Gilliam, I am beginning to wonder if you are pulling back from me a bit. . . .

I read Simon's latest e-mail in disbelief.

He had to be kidding! Did he not just tell me—after a period of calling me innumerable times, sending me love poems he'd written, and glance-dancing with me in sanctuaries, pool halls, his kitchen, and friends' homes—that he was uncertain about his timeline but knew he'd be moving all the way across the country soon, to be gone for an undetermined period? Had he not made it clear that he was in no position to get involved in any kind of set (read: committed) relationship? "Of course, you moron," I wanted to scream. "Of course I'm pulling back! Hello! What is your major malfunction? This is what I have to contend with—from grown men who have good jobs, own their homes, and are decent looking. Agh!"

Suddenly my mind flashed back to the time when Hank Roberts, my on-again, off-again crush, had looked me up after breaking up with his longtime girlfriend. When he had given me a rather electrifying surprise kiss after dinner, I (albeit reluctantly) pulled back and said, "Uh, Hank. You can't do that."

"Why?" he asked.

"Because you just broke up with your girlfriend, and you said you are really upset about her."

I remember his look of genuine confusion as he replied, "What does *she* have to do with *you and me*?" In Hank's mind, his ex-girlfriend and his relationship with her were in a totally different category from Hank and me. He'd been "honest" with me about her, so what was the problem?

Now here I was again, faced with Simon who, having been "honest" that he was probably moving and had no intention of pursuing anything definitive with me, felt disturbed because I was "pulling back." With Hank, the shocking logic had surfaced right in my foyer, and with his handsome face peering into mine. I had just barely survived. However, with Simon simply on my computer screen—and with a few more years of older women's wisdom ("You have to teach men everything") under my belt—I decided that Simon was not a bad guy. Maybe instead of hostility, I should try and help the man understand.

Sitting on my sofa that night I reread the paper printout of Simon's e-mail. Staring at it, I tried to pin down what it was I wanted to say in response to him. Sighing, I realized that I had no clue what the truth was. With my feet propped up on the coffee table, I threw back my head and sighed, "Oh God, help me to know what to say to this guy."

Slowly, a conversation from seven or eight years prior crept back into my mind. Gwen, a friend in Philly, had pointed me to a quote from the Old Testament book of love poetry, Song of Songs. It read, "You are a garden locked up, my sister, my bride; you are a spring enclosed, a sealed fountain."[6] She'd read that to me because I, like a number of my girlfriends, suffered from the chronic "Oh, Please, Handsome (or Handsome Enough) Man, Come In and Love Me" Syndrome. This disease had often left our hearts unlocked, unsealed, and disappointed. There is such a thing as *too open*.

But as quickly as I remembered that quote, I also thought back further, to fifteen years before, when I was in college. My roommates and I had laughed reading a passage from one friend's textbook for her "History of Virginia" class. The book quoted a nineteenth-century writer who had commented that spending an evening with a Virginia Presbyterian girl (which described me) was something akin to sitting on an iceberg, chipping hailstones with his teeth. How was one to be a sealed-up garden without becoming the ice castle queen?

At this point, I must interject that I never imagined I'd be in my thirties having to ask myself these questions. As a little girl, I figured I'd grow up and get married like, well, just like everyone else. My grandmother once explained to me that in my first year of college I was supposed to date lots of boys. My sophomore year was about figuring out which one I really liked and eventually dating him exclusively. My junior year, I was to get him to pin me. And my senior year, we would get engaged. My mother and aunt had followed not dissimilar patterns themselves, and things seemed to work out well for them. So, sitting on that sofa, I found myself scratching my head wondering if the right gene had skipped my DNA.

Regardless, I knew that I now needed to find the elusive balance between being a fortress on one hand and an amusement park on the other, and God only knew—literally—how to navigate that in-beween land. My mind wandered back to that Song of Songs imagery. A walled garden. Perhaps it wasn't the same thing as a frigid castle. While someone or something had thoroughly deconstructed just about every approach to relationships for me over the years, I decided to risk leaning on that ancient, inspired garden metaphor.

Grabbing my laptop and settling into the crook of the sofa's arm, I began to type. After a few false starts, this emerged:

> *Okay, Simon. Please let me explain something. You are right when you sense that I am "pulling back," but I'd like to take a minute to explain. See, Simon, a woman's heart is a lot like a garden. There are, in the garden, public areas. This is where almost anyone can traverse (read: decent colleagues, the kind checker at the grocery store, the rare person on the subway who gives up his or her seat, neighbors who want to borrow a tool, parents of friends, little kids in the park, etc.). Then there is the center of her garden. It's a special place, reserved ultimately for the person who wants to commit to "husband her garden permanently," so to speak. (I know you're into etymology, Simon. I guess you know that the word husband actually is an agricultural term.)*
>
> *Anyhow, the tricky part, of course, is that there's this in-between place, somewhere between the inner sanctum and the outer ring, and that's where this gets all confusing. Basically, Simon, the folks I let into this more fluid in-between part are some key family members, longtime girlfriends, a few guys I consider brothers, my boss who I know cares for me, and guys who are interested in exploring the idea of entering into that inner sanctum. The problem, Simon, is that once a guy whom I like—and Simon, I have felt chemistry between us—decides he's not particularly interested in long-term inner sanctum husbandry, I can't let him wander all around the middle ground anymore. If I do, then he inevitably crosses lines he doesn't know he's crossing, and I inevitably try to pull him into the center. He can't figure out why I'm all upset (because, after all, he was honest about his lack of intentions), and I keep hoping I'm going to change him. That, Simon, is a recipe for disaster.*
>
> *So, brother Simon, that's the scoop. I hope this helps. I do care about*

you, and I want you in my public areas, so to speak. But in light of
everything you've said, for now, that's all I can invite.

I exhaled and reread. Taking a very deep breath, I reread again, and
then I hit the very scary "Send" button. "Your message has been sent"
danced across the screen. "Oh well, who knows? Hope this does
something good for somebody." Getting up off the sofa, I went to eat
some Ben and Jerry's New York Super Fudge Chunk before going for
a power walk. Surprisingly, I felt calm.

Had that been the end of the story, it would have been a decent
ending simply because articulating all those things about the garden
of my heart was a good exercise for me. In the struggle, I finally found
language, however limited, to explain my heart to a man. But amazingly, something more happened. About twenty minutes after I got
home from my walk, the phone rang. It was Simon, wanting—of all
things—to thank me.

"Connally, you are the first woman who has ever explained what
was going on in her mind without going psycho on me. Thank you.
That really helped me understand."

For one moment, I thought, *This can't be. He can't really mean that this is all*
new to him. The man is over forty years old. No wonder women have gone all psycho
on him. And then, for reasons I could not even identify at the time, I
pushed all those thoughts aside and said, "You're welcome, Simon. I
hope it helps." It was a strange moment, a rare moment of letting go of
my expectations that somehow men should intrinsically know how to
be good men and women should know how to be good women and we
should all know how to be good to each other. It was a moment of letting go of my consistently-proved-false-but-tenaciously-insistent illusion that Mr. 100-Percent-Right was out there waiting to spar, laugh,
and instantly connect with me. And it was a moment of tasting, if just
for a fleeting instant, the good in helping a guy grow.

After that, Simon and I chatted on for a while, declaring our mutual admiration (there was lots to appreciate about Simon) but also quietly putting to rest that toxic pressure that ping-pongs misfit couples back and forth between "You owe me" and "Don't demand from me." Simon did not change his mind and decide to vie once again for the keys to the inner sanctum, nor did I ask him to. We agreed that we'd just try to be as normal as ever with one another—whatever that would mean.

My wiser, older friend Jennifer once used another metaphor when explaining relationships to me. "Men," she said, "are like houses. There is no perfect one out there. Eventually you pick one you really like and settle in, knowing you'll be doing home improvements for the rest of your life." When she first said it, it sounded depressing. I wanted one of those old and solid but completely redone homes. The kind that is highlighted in *Architectural Digest*. High ceilings, crown molding, wood floors, stainless steel kitchen appliances. You know, the basics. Not something that was going to take fixing up.

After my experience with Simon, however, my perspective began to change. I discovered, albeit amid awkwardness, disappointment, and even laughter, that home improvements can actually be gratifying. Seriously. Perhaps you hear the hesitation or touch of disbelief in my voice. It is there. I hear it myself. Somewhere along the line, I inadvertently bought into the notion that to help a man grow is to make myself shrink, in the worst, shriveled-doormat sense of that word, and the shadow of that mistaken thinking still lingers. But with Simon, I discovered instead that it is a very fine thing to help a grateful guy grow.

Of course, it also would be wonderful to have someone really commit to trying to care for the garden of my heart. I can finally own and explain this without being a bumbling, defensive mess. But putting aside for a minute that question of a mate, I am simply glad to have tasted what it is to help a guy better understand and appreciate us women. In and of itself, it is a savory taste, not completely foreign and very delicious. It is a taste that now lingers with me, and honestly, I am hoping for a second helping.

CHAPTER 5

I Just Gotta Be Queen

Sometimes being unintentionally single can leave a woman feeling socially out of place, a bit adrift in the swirl of opportunities, and as if she's constantly striving to protect the garden of her own heart. This is reality. However, as is obvious to most onlookers, there are also a lot of pluses at work. Barbra Dafoe Whitehead, in her book *Why There Are No Good Men Left*, suggests that women born since the mid-sixties were raised to be independent achievers. She says we're like "specimen orchids . . . bred to win prizes."[7] And many of us do have the education, the savvy, and the presence to live like those orchids: beautiful and freestanding, regardless of the men and marriage issue. In that sense, we have this unusual opportunity to live as victim or victor, or genuinely a little of both.

But in bouncing between these two poles, I've seen there's still more to the story. And it is worth mentioning, if for no other reason than to round out the picture. In short, whether we're well-bred or-chids, wilting violets, or hybrids, none of us—if you'll pardon the cliché—smells entirely like a rose. Actually, this journey as a single woman—perhaps like the journey of every human being—has re-vealed in me, to put it unpoetically, my inner stink.

Growing up with Southern roots, "nice" was a value woven into just about every imaginable aspect of my female life. To be a "nice girl" was a high, if oxymoronic, value. How could someone who, in order to embrace her faith, had to own the dark shadows resident in her heart then be expected to be chronically nice? That question aside, however . . . In practice, being nice meant wearing nice clothes (taste-ful, pressed, and stylish), using nice words (which excluded more than just your basic four-letter words), having nice friends (from nice fami-lies), and using nice manners. "You catch more flies with honey than with vinegar" and "Pretty is as pretty does" were axioms lodged in my brain before I could speak. If you have lived in this culture—or bumped up against it—you know something of which I speak. You might also imagine what a shock it was to me when I discovered that, in spite of what the culture around me championed as the supreme virtue—to be combined, of course, with education, social grace, and confidence—there were parts of my core self that were not nice, not even remotely nice.

Of course, I'm always tempted to blame the people around me for the existence of my inner stink, because generally it is when I'm with *people* (versus trees or squirrels) that the ugly parts of me emerge. The warmth of relating to men, women, and children up close, which is what I love and long for, can become the very fire that smokes out the ugly little Gollum hiding in the dark caverns of my heart.

Perhaps because I've had fourteen of them (twenty-eight if you include college and grad school), I've seen this most acutely with my roommates. Of course, this includes assorted group-living situa-tions, so it has not meant twenty-eight different sets of coordinated bedspreads or impossibly tiny, shared closet spaces. But it has meant lots of working through who will buy the bananas, who will pay the phone bill, and who will clean the toilets. Inevitably, this has meant conflict.

One roommate, Sandi, and I had so much tension that we really about killed each other. In short, before we embarked on the awkward and unpracticed work of conflict resolution, there were moments when I fantasized about running my car keys down the side of her shiny blue sports car. That's not nice. Simultaneously, she mentioned wanting at one point to shake me "until [my] teeth fell out." That's not nice either. Another roommate, Maria, and I once stood on a street corner and, uncharacteristically, let each other have it. I don't really remember the words we screamed (our different racial backgrounds, combined with the shared compulsion to mask mistrust and arrogance under niceness, played into it). But though the spewing was a good thing, like opening a festering wound, the public display wasn't pretty. The ladies strolling with babies in their carriages were suddenly scurrying for shelter.

This ugly side of me, however, hasn't just popped up in a few tense moments. No, I've realized it is often bubbling beneath the surface like a leak in the sewer. Nothing is dramatically visible, but something doesn't smell right.

Sitting over omelets at the diner, a friend buttered her toast and said, "You're competitive, aren't you?"

"Uh . . . what? . . . Well, maybe, well . . ." It struck me as a comment out of thin air. She wasn't talking about a competitive nature that simply shows up on the tennis court or the putt-putt course (and why I'm competitive in putt-putt beats me; I'm pitiful). She was making a far bigger statement.

"Yeah, I can tell you're competitive," she said, as if she could smell it.

For a nice girl like me, this comment—except in the appropriate spheres such as sports or job responsibilities—was an automatic "flag." But I wasn't about to get penalized and lose the "I'm really the nicest and deepest and most understanding person around" game, at least not without a fight. So, I cheekily jabbed back.

"Takes one to know one, eh?"

I wish instead I had smiled, said, "Yep," and asked her why she mentioned it.

Actually, competition born of my desire to *do my best* can be a great and motivating force. But it also has a shadow side. Its Mr. Hyde is my need to *be better than you*. When I switched careers to intentionally work with female peers, this lurking and strangely dark side surfaced. It's one thing to be engaged in coaching and developing significantly younger people. It's a delightful thing—bringing out the nurturing, maternal side of me. But it was a completely different scenario when, in the context of this new job, I had to think of my peers—the former competition, if you will—as women to serve. Imagine gathering a small group of your same-sex peers. All are single, attractive, vocationally successful, and desirous of hooking one of the few eligible bachelors in your area. Historically, my unspoken strategic goal would have been to compare and contrast, to sort and select, to politely size up the competition. It sounds horrible, shallow, and superficial. But it was, and still can be, me.

Having to view the hopes, dreams, and desires of these women through the lens of *service* versus *competition* was nothing short of painful. To stop asking, *What can I get from this?* and start asking, *What can I give?* felt like someone was reaching down into my guts, ripping out deeply entrenched infrastructure, and leaving me hollow, with only a few lone truths to lean on. As one woman would tell a tale of some on-again, off-again interlude with an eligible man, I would find myself having to intentionally *just say no* to the old, familiar "jealousy of others' joys," as one friend calls it. Otherwise, I couldn't ask myself the necessary questions, like *What could help this woman as she looks for wisdom?* or *What does it sound like her next step might be?* But for the longest period, all such interactions left me feeling like a part of me was dying. And it did not, at least at the time, feel good.

But I'm getting ahead of myself.

Really, I'm talking about something deeper than behavior or behavior modification. Actions and impulses are just where this deeper garbage shows up. What's at the core is some sewer that just keeps leaking, and for the life of me, all the well-intentioned plumbing work can't stop it. I feel with Paul when he says, "I do not understand what I do. For what I want to do I do not do, but what I hate I do."[8]

I feel, too, with my friend Caroline. She has been candid with me about the codependent path she traveled in an unhealthy female friendship. On one hand, something in her knew the friendship was amiss. That fact gnawed at her. But her basic instinct for connection with another person was powerfully compelling. It seemed to fuzz her very sense of right and wrong, healthy and diseased. So even if it meant playing mental games and twisting her conscience, satisfying the instinct-turned-craving felt worth it. She explained it this way:

> There's the emptiness of my heart that wants oneness with
> another person. I want someone to do life with, [someone to]
> share meals, grocery shopping, days off, errands with—I want
> to get home at the end of the day and have someone to eat
> with, watch movies with. I've always known I really wanted
> a husband to do this with, but with no man in the picture,
> a woman felt almost right.

Why is it that we're so willing, as C. S. Lewis once wrote, to trade a holiday at the seashore for a day spent making mud pies?[9] Sometimes it is because we can't currently see the seashore, so we don't believe it is there. Or, if we do, we just don't trust *we* will ever get to go to the seashore. As a result, though our desires can be for good things, and we might even have a true inkling of where those good things are

found, we can put all that aside in a flash. Instead, we make ourselves—our feelings, our impulses, and perhaps most significantly,
our limited perspectives—the center of the universe. Making ourselves the center of the universe seems to be the source of our great
stink.

My friend Steph knows what I'm talking about. Reflecting on the
shadowy side of her own heart, she writes:

> Have I seen the dark/shady/ugly side of my heart? Of course!
> On the metro, my reactions to strangers—disdain, judgment,
> jealousy. In the car, the amount of anger I experience toward
> someone who cuts me off or even because of slow traffic—like
> a dragon waiting to be unleashed. Within my family and
> friendships on a day-to-day basis—my impatience, my me-
> first attitude, my unwillingness to give. My snubbing of those
> I consider in some way inferior or beneath me. In my prayer
> life—the number of prayers that revolve simply around me
> and my desires. In my lust for more of everything—
> more things, more pleasure, more fulfillment, more attention,
> more recognition. Me, me, me, me. Isn't that the darkest/
> ugliest/shadiest side? The biggest lie I think we all believe is
> that "it's all about me."

I read Steph's words and know they are tough. But do they energize you like they energize me? She's passionate in calling things
straight, and somehow her words free me to shelve the numbing illusions of fundamental niceness. Something in me exhales.

Ultimately, I've had no choice but to discover the sewer from
which all this muck leaks: my small but relentlessly insidious impulse
to be queen (dare I say *god*?). First, though, let me clarify. I'm not talking about wanting to be a real queen with responsibilities to think first
of serving her subjects. That sounds far too much like work! Nor am I

thinking of Leonardo DiCaprio in *Titanic*. His acting might have been questionable, but when he stood out on the bow of the ship, arms outspread, yelling, "I'm the king of the world!" there was something in his exclamation that was an expression of joy, a feeling that life couldn't get better. I think every human being alive must yearn to slip into such a royal and glorious robe of delight.

No, I'm talking about a force within—the inner stink—that quietly over time or perhaps in a flash, with a touch of Shakespearean drama, proclaims—*God, I bite my thumb at thee!* The inner stink that, with the fallen angel of Milton's *Paradise Lost*, declares, "Better to reign in hell than serve in heaven." Have you ever shared those fallen angel thoughts? I have.

Remember my roommate Sandi whose car I wanted to scratch? She had a small poster in her bedroom. The photo escapes me, but the words remain emblazoned in my mind: *There is a God. You are not him.* I loved that poster because it cut to the chase. And there is something about calling things as they really are that is incredibly life-giving. At the University of Virginia, where I went to school, one of the old buildings is engraved with this motto: "You shall know the truth and the truth shall set you free." I think the designers really knew what they were doing when they borrowed these words of Jesus.

That's a big part of the reason I even mention these things. Some people get a kick out of talking about bad smells and dark shadows. I don't. But if the truth can help shed some light on our sewer problems or if it can release in someone else freedom, joy, or Life with a capital *L*, as it keeps doing in me, then it's worth exposing the "nice" myth and putting it in its rightful place.

Liz, a journalism grad student in Philadelphia, puts it this way:

> Understanding my [heart] can be like trying to sort out a very dimly lit closet. I desire to see what is there, to make sense of what needs to be gotten rid of and what should be kept. But

the dimness of the light makes it very hard to see what's what
. . . and easy to hold up something ugly, but sort of talk myself
into believing it's something good. The best intimate
relationships help shed light into that closet.

Actually, Caroline said it's that shed light of truth that helped her
snap out of her relational fog and codependency. She shared this
analogy (borrowed and changed, she admits, from author/pastor John
Piper):

It was as if I'd been searching for a piece of precious black
ivory. Walking into a darkened room, I stumbled upon
something that glinted, a shiny bit of black. Picking it up, I
stroked it, held it to my cheek, and thought I'd found my
prize. Then a friend came into the room and threw on the
light switch. Suddenly, I realized I was holding a large and
shiny roach.

In short, even though the doors of our culture have been thrown
wide open for single women to live economically self-sufficient, socially independent, and sexually liberated lives,[10] we still need help
honestly naming and reckoning with that inner "I just gotta be queen"
impulse. Actually, come to think of it, maybe it's *precisely because* those
doors have been thrown wide open, allowing us to live autono-
mously—with fewer constraints, authority, and limits than ever before—that we need help like never before. We've got to get the light
thrown on or otherwise we might all end up petting roaches, so to
speak.

Frederica Mathewes-Green notes in her essay "Twice Liberated: A
Personal Journey through Feminism" that sometimes it is hard for men
and women to acknowledge *in women* this ugly side, but in failing to do
so, we chain women to pedestals. (As an aside, a pedestal is the perfect

place to display a prizewinning, if solitary, orchid.) But Mathewes-Green laments this, proposing that it actually demeans women to disallow them membership in what is sometimes considered an "all-male club," a club into which are lumped the twisted, foggy, jealous, and self-centered. She writes, "While women and men have many delightful differences, there is one item we indisputably share. 'All have sinned and fallen short of the glory of God.'"[11]

Mathewes-Green, quoting Paul, gets it so right. Male and female alike, our inner stink, our leaky sewer lines, our shadows, our sin—whatever you want to call it—naturally messes us up in relation to God and others. And the results, as I keep seeing, are not pretty.

For example, if my "I just gotta be queen" impulse is reigning, then it's a bit like practicing divine identity fraud. I take God's ID card, resources, and decision-making power to use for my purposes. I play god in my life and sometimes the lives of others. Then I start running and spend the rest of my life hoping like mad that the real God never catches up with me. Somehow I suspect that if he does, he's not going to be happy with me. After all, would you be? No. Justifiably indignant would probably be an understatement. What a mess.

The "I just gotta be queen" stink also creates issues, because most of us—okay, all of us—are sorry little gods. Have you seen the movie *Bruce Almighty?* I thought it was a fun movie, but it humorously crushed any illusion that Me Almighty or [Your Name Here] Almighty could do a better job. If anyone has ever asked you, "So, who died and made you God?" you know it's not said because you are a delightful, life-giving resource to those around you. To the contrary. People offer such comments when just the smell of your or my presumed "I think I'm God" attitude leaks into our relationships.

Most profoundly, however, the "I just gotta be queen" life breaks God's heart and ultimately will break, or harden, ours. While it might sound like a religious cliché, God decidedly yearns for the hearts of people. He doesn't just want to see people like you and me respecting his identity or relating to others with humility (though both have inestimable value). Rather, he passionately pursues our hearts, with a self-giving love that only he, the real God of the universe, can provide. So when we, in a fit of self-reign, tell God to "talk to the hand," so to speak, we are actually holding at bay a profoundly rich and real love. Hence, when we fall short of the glory of God, it's not just that we fail to measure up, which we do. But we also lose out. Picture someone running to catch a much sought-after bus. At the last minute, she trips over her own royal robes and falls, just short of the bus. It pulls away. A good thing lost.

Talking about this idea of a divine love that could be known were she to relinquish her royal robes, my friend Melissa said it appealed on some level. But on another level, it scared her to death. She didn't want anyone else—God included—reigning, or in some way possessing, her heart. In Melissa's paradigm, to have one's heart possessed by God meant losing all autonomy. Given that choice, she'd gladly choose self-rule. As we talked, I tried to explain how God's loving reign mysteriously begets more freedom in our hearts—that as we lose our lives to his loving possession, we gain them and are empowered in far richer ways than we can imagine. But this paradox is sometimes hard to accept.

What's encouraging in all of this, however, is that in spite of any of our impulses toward being queen, God is relentlessly committed to seeing each of us freed to love and live well. The inner stink, with its related shadow and loss, does not have to dictate the end of the story. Instead, the real story seems to begin in earnest when we can acknowledge that though many of us are prizewinning orchids standing amid winds of cultural change, we are not the center of the universe. Or, put another way, maybe the best story of a single woman's life should begin this way: "Once upon a time there a little girl who did *not* grow up to be queen."

CHAPTER 6

Men—Who Needs Them?

It's an interesting question: *Who needs men?* Over the past few years I have been asking single friends—and myself—this question or ones like it. And the answers I've received have ranged from the poetic to the perfunctory. Said one friend, "I need the deep groundedness of their bass and tenor voices in my life . . . it helps me catch the tune of my own feminine voice." Another honestly reflected, "You know, as independent, capable, self-sufficient, driven, and butterfly-ish as I am, I definitely need men. Or at least, I feel like I need *one* man." Still another wrote, "I do not need a man." Her tenor wasn't harsh, just direct. She continued, "I have built a life for myself that involves some close girlfriends and a large circle of acquaintances, and I have a job I love and think I'm pretty good at. It pretty much allows me a lifestyle that is comfortable and has quite a number of perks." Another self-revealing friend responded, "I don't need them to pay my rent, change the oil in my car, move furniture, or mow the lawn (although all that would be nice). [But] I feel most like a woman when I'm with a man."

In most of the single women I know, there is a residual sense of needing men, at least on some level. And yet in practice, there's a lot of life—like paying rent and changing oil and cutting grass—that can be lived without them. As a result, I've seen in many twenty- and thirty-something single women a strange ambivalence around this question: Who needs men?

Sometimes I wonder if it is, in part, a problem of the words we use. While I've not found anyone who thinks it's wrong or abnormal to *desire* a man—or the company of men—there is often an unspoken caveat. It is fine to desire from a place of internal strength, but when it is desire that's born of *need*, somehow, well . . . that's just a little sketchy. Maybe it's some of the circles I've run in or into, but somehow *needing* a man seems to quietly connote an undue weakness or potential desperation (i.e., being sort of *needy*). Citing the best-selling book *The Rules*, Barbara Dafoe Whitehead offers a picture of the new ideal single woman: "You are a very fulfilled person—stable, functional, and happy—with a career, friends, and hobbies . . . and you are perfectly capable of living with or without him. You are not an empty vessel waiting for him to fill you up, support you, or give you a life."[12] No, this is not a woman with evident needs.

A leader whom I respect tremendously once commented, "You know, nothing scares men away like a needy or desperate woman." So, as there's this very fine (to the point of being almost invisible) line between *needing* and being *needy*, I see many friends conclude that perhaps the best thing a woman can do is to cultivate an air of detachment around the whole topic of needing men. "While a man in my life would be nice for a couple of reasons, I can do it on my own." Any deeper or more potent desire for a special man, let alone men in general, gets swallowed. Perhaps, in fairness, this is because the question of what to do with such a desire is swamped in ambiguity. You can't purchase the love of your life, and you can't make your male friends or colleagues come around you in the ways you need. So wisdom seems to dictate holding your cards close to your chest until, well, until they disappear.

The unfortunate irony, however, is that in my world I hear numerous comments from men bemoaning women's self-sufficiency. I have heard many males utter some form of the phrase, "Women don't need us anymore; we've become obsolete." Have you heard this too? And is it true? Have men become obsolete from your vantage point? Honestly, for many of us, the need deficit is a reality. For example, do we need men for financial provision? We might like it, but it's not crucial. Do we need men for physical protection? Perhaps when walking to a car late at night, but generally we live in a world governed by the rule of law, and that's enough. How about social status? Of course, no one wants to be excluded from dinner parties because she lacks a man, but at least in metropolitan areas, social opportunities decidedly exist for single women. How about emotional connection? Don't we expect our girlfriends to fill a lot of these gaps? Kids? We can adopt or be artificially inseminated. The only obvious thing left is sex, which some women are content to live without or embrace in such a way that no meaningful, lasting relationship with a man is necessary. In short, men on the whole aren't *really* needed any longer, at least not in the clear-cut ways of previous generations.

Perhaps part of the ensuing ambivalence about *needing men* is that what many single women find themselves actually left wanting and what many men find themselves capable of offering are more divergent than ever. The language of so many of my single girlfriends is the vocabulary of "connection" and "soul mates." Launched in good careers and already owning condos, but living in transient communities without extended families, many in this group yearn for intimacy. It's something that even from a point of strength we can't create on our own.

Ironically, this intimacy is something that a largely unfathered generation of men seems, on the whole, least prepared to offer. It is not so much that these men lack language for their feelings or are sexually impotent; there are plenty of twenty- and thirty-something single men who can say "I feel angry" or "I feel lonely" or who can bed a woman with ease. More significantly, many lack the conviction, confidence, and capacity to commit to creating the structures (i.e., marriage and family) that have nurtured and sustained intimacy over the ages. So the women are longing, and in some cases dying, for intimacy. And the men are clueless as to how to help build it.

Once, when speaking on a panel about singleness to a group of about sixty adults ranging in age and marital status, I listened as a seventy-ish widower reflected on his experience. I was struck—astounded, actually—by the clarity of the respective needs prompting and characterizing his and his wife's marriage and life together. As a young man captured by the beauty of a young woman, he'd confidently offered the things this young woman wanted: love, complete fidelity, financial provision, and fatherhood to their children. In exchange, also loving him, she had borne and raised the children, shouldered responsibility for the home (keeping the fridge stocked, his shirts pressed, and the flowers growing in the garden), all while weaving her husband into a larger network of friends. He recalled, "I was so lost when she died. I didn't know how to function." Predictably, I thought he was referring to some deep emotional pain, but he was referring to buying his own groceries and making his way to the dry cleaner's. Then, reflecting further for a moment and choking back tears, he continued, "She taught me about love. She became my best friend."

What struck me about his story was the order or structure implicit in his reflections. In addition to the adrenaline of sharing a mutual love, evident and seemingly meet-able needs spurred this couple into marriage. That confident commitment created a context for this man (and presumably his wife) to discover and value, over the course of many years, what a number of my friends and I have assumed to be an up-front nonnegotiable: intimacy with a soul mate. But with both clear-cut needs and the confidence to meet the remaining felt needs waning, it is no wonder that I hear confessions like that of one twenty-something Washington, DC, man: "Women are mad at us for not being the men they want us to be, but we don't even know what it is to be men, let alone how to get there or offer women what they want."

With exceptions, the previous generations' blueprints for dating, marriage, and simple opposite-sex relating seem to fit fewer single people's life experience today. And now that more of us can bring home our personal bacon *and* fry it up in a pan, and since intimacy seems elusive, the question for single women returns. Do women genuinely need men?

Perhaps because of the culture of privilege that characterizes much of the United States, my first memory of experiencing a real and objective need for men—a need deeper than just a vague ache, a flash of desire, or an impulse for social normalcy—came at age thirty-one, in another country. I was on a train in India. Being led to my destination by a Hindi-speaking male who communicated via warm nods and animated body language, I was traveling in the coed train car. (There were "women only" train cars in Bombay, but not knowing when to get off the train, I had to stick with my guide.)

As we rode in that all-male-except-for-me train car, I found myself standing a head above a sea of Indian men whose bodies were smashed up against mine. Not convinced that the rule of law had any particular power in these men's lives, I suddenly found myself profoundly grateful to be with my guide. Though he was half a foot shorter than I, his presence next to me communicated, "Do not bother this woman." The glances he shot in the direction of those who leered hungrily in my direction felt like arrows shot on my behalf. At that moment, I could not contemplate being without him; I knew I needed him.

Likewise, when my younger brother arrived in India a week later from his home in the Middle East, something that was unwittingly clenched in me exhaled. One of the friends I'd made in the interim said to me, "Your face is much more relaxed now that your brother is here." Though something within me flinched at his words (my illusion of self-sufficiency had taken a blow), my face told the real story: at the reflex level, my brother's presence, like that of the guide but with a further and deeper reach, carried with it the power to bring me to a place of rest which, at least in that culture, I couldn't get to on my own. I genuinely needed his presence.

Over the past decade, I've been looking for moments reminiscent of those Indian experiences. I have found a few; the closest ones have been primarily physical in nature. Having moved four times, I've needed muscles to lift pianos, sofa beds, and endless boxes of books. Short on cash and replete with girlfriends who would rather help pack, I've needed the men in my life to step up. And a few times, when I've just been too weary for more confrontation, different men have, sometimes at their initiative and sometimes at my invitation, stepped in and fought for me (with the computer manufacturer, the car mechanic, etc.). Still, I theoretically could have hired someone to do these things or simply found more girlfriends with greater upper-body strength.

Plus, something about my brother's presence was different from simply the presence of a bodyguard or a beloved sister with biceps. Something less tangible, but decidedly peace giving.

In the mid-nineties, Whitney Houston and Angela Bassett starred in the movie *Waiting to Exhale*. "Four friends," the trailer says, "are determined to face reality." Inevitably, facing reality means facing their relationships with men. While the movie ultimately champions the strength gained from female friendships and highlights the capacity of men to create real problems, what caught my attention were the few brief "good men" moments. When Savannah (Houston) slow dances with a man, she is for that moment able to let go, to stop being "on." Later in the movie, Bernadine (Bassett) falls asleep in the comforting presence of a man who simply cares for her well at the right time (admittedly, the audience does have to suspend some disbelief). Though small glimmers in the movie, something in each of these moments is reminiscent of that same mysterious gift I tasted in India. One glimpses men enabling the women to exhale.

Recently, I attended a Valentine's Day dinner at the home of a friend I affectionately call Bald Harry (he shaves his head). The men who organized the event did the inviting, setting up, cooking, and serving. Dinner concluded with Harry's brave recitation (brave because of the slightly bemused snickers of the other men, which actually seemed to embolden him) from Longfellow's nineteenth-century epic poem "The Courtship of Miles Standish." Interestingly, it is a tale of a man who has no language for the deepest part of his heart. The poem lingered in the air a few moments—perhaps many of us, men and women alike, have lost language for our deepest longings—and then, after a short, Harry-led prayer, the men transformed the dining area into a dance floor, and most of us made our way onto it.

There was no budding romance for me that evening. Nor was I in any danger from which I needed protection. And even the physical labor that needed doing wasn't much—with so many hands at work, a group of women easily could have knocked it out. But nevertheless, that same "India thing" transpired. That evening, I found myself exhaling. Somehow in their planning, serving, risking, and engaging, that motley crew of men helped my omnicompetence find a temporary shelf. It wasn't a starry or dreamy night, but I left with the gift of rest, mysteriously provided by the presence of this hodgepodge of brothers.

Could I have lived without that Valentine's dinner? Yes. Did I decidedly need those men that night? No, not really. Honestly, I've lived through a lot of single Valentine's Day dinners and have had both lonely and laughter-ridden times with friends. But nevertheless, those men's offerings and simple presence touched something in me, and it was good. I left wondering, *What exactly is that thing that men have that we need?* Honestly, it's hard to define, but you know it when you smell it.

My friend Liz tells this story. Sure, it's a reflection not just of men but of her personality, but she gets at some of what I'm trying to say. She'd just returned from a hard Christmas with her mom and sister, and having broken up with her fiancé in the fall, she was making her own New Year's plans. She decided on a dinner party.

> I knew of a few single women that I would invite. But I decided I really wanted to have some men at the table. Since most of the single men I know are connected [with my ex-fiancé], I wound up inviting three married couples and two single girlfriends. One of the couples couldn't come, but the other two did.
>
> I often approach dinner parties with an eye to make deep and meaningful conversation happen. With the kind of year I'd had, I didn't have the energy to do that for this dinner party. But it turned out to be a wonderful evening. One of the couples brought a game they'd received for Christmas, and we played that for a while. But the best part was when the whole group got into a conversation about safety procedures on airlines (one of the couples had flown over the holiday). I laughed so hard I was sore when I woke up the next day! Now, if that evening had been just the single women in my life, I would have felt sort of compelled to steer conversation in that deep, meaningful, probing direction. But what I really needed that night was to laugh and play and just enjoy the diversity of a group of friends. Having men at the table helped make that possible.

Maybe it seems obvious that there's some mysterious offering good men can provide—a space to breathe? a sparkle?—yet it is so hard to nail down. And some women just flat-out disagree, a fact I was recently reminded of by a bumper sticker that read: "A woman needs a man like a fish needs a bicycle."

It's at this point that I find myself thrown back to Scripture and its first mention of people, of men and women. The first chapter of Genesis reads: "God created man in His own image, in the image of God He created him; male and female He created them."[13] Since the nineteenth century, these and related passages have been used consistently by assorted biblical scholars to highlight the equality of women with men, the distinct identity that women possess as image bearers of God, and the implicit character traits of God that we typically refer to as feminine. Debates have swirled around these issues, and most likely will continue to do so. However, I've found myself coming to this text from the other side of the page.

Not so consumed with the place of women in culture—rather, wondering more about the role men play—I've reflected on this passage. Again, it might seem obvious, but my conclusion is that men and women, together, reflect God's image. That's why both genders are flooded with value. And it's why we need each other. Even if you or I lack any practical, urgent, or felt need for men, men—as equal image bearers of God—are integral to our knowing, seeing, and experiencing *him*. So, though it may be a mystery, somehow men and women do need each other, working together like an eagle with the sky or a ship with the high seas. Maybe in our strange new culture, fish actually do need bicycles.

In the past, women were propelled into interdependent relationships with men to a far greater degree than they are today. Perhaps many women exercised the strange privilege of jokingly (and sometimes not-so-jokingly) reducing men to "overeating lugs who happen to father our children," while still receiving and enjoying the benefits of God's image, imperfectly present in those males. In other words, it was fine to devalue men—or play the game of one-upmanship—because as far as anyone could see, men and women were stuck with each other. I say this cautiously, recognizing my own naïveté and ignorance about fallen men, abusive relationships, and oppressive social structures. Undeniably, relative to most women in the world and in history, I speak from a place of freedom. But it is precisely that freedom (i.e., we are no longer stuck with men) that demands of my peers and me both a decision and a discovery: Will we choose to believe that men carry the image of God? And if so, will we risk discovering more of what the image looks like in a handful of assorted fathers, brothers, colleagues, friends, and, potentially, a husband?

Believing and discovering is a risk, because men—like women—are fallen image bearers and can be schmucks as fathers, brothers, colleagues, friends, or husbands, and more often than not as strangers. They can spark deep, angry breaths and elicit sad, weary sighs. The contemporary context for so many educated, single women living in urban areas and working professional jobs is so different from that of the seventy-ish widower's I mentioned earlier. Because of this, I proceed in both life and in this chapter with a hefty backdrop of prayer and humility.

But what I've discovered—beyond the endless if necessary debates around gender roles and traits, and beyond the disappointments I've experienced—is the relentless truth about the mysterious but real offering of *male* men. I say mysterious because it's hard to define. It is like the blowing of the wind. I can't put the offering in a box; I can't measure its edges; but I can tell when it's blowing by its effect on me. In my case, something mysterious transpires, and a part of me exhales, perhaps in proportion to the depth of care accompanying the offered strength.

Put more concretely, my friend Cindi says it this way: "Think about getting a compliment from a woman versus getting the same compliment from a man. It's different. Think about a girlfriend walking you to your car or a guy walking you to your car. That's different." Those examples may sound silly, but I think there's something there.

No doubt many women, perhaps including you, will discover the image of God revealed in men in a variety of forms. Clearly, my experience, just like those of Liz or Cindi or a host of other friends, is shaped by a particular context and personality. But because God's image, although blurred, universally resides in men, there *is* an answer to the question *Who needs men?* And while the answer is only a starting place and begs another host of questions that this chapter doesn't address, it is nevertheless an answer on which we can solidly stand.

Who needs men? I'd humbly venture to say *we all do.*

CHAPTER 7

Freedom!

Do you remember the 1999 Women's World Cup at the Rose Bowl in Pasadena, California? The championship soccer game—watched by 40 million viewers in this country alone—came down to a shoot-out after two sudden death overtimes. USA's Brandi Chastain hit the game-winning shot past China's goalkeeper, and while the stadium erupted with the cheers of ninety thousand fans, Brandi, in the tradition of many male soccer players before her, ripped off her jersey, awaited her rushing teammates, and gracefully fell to her knees. The motion instantly propelled her into a dramatic media spotlight. When later asked why she threw off her shirt, she girlishly attributed it to the "momentary insanity" into which she and the crowds were catapulted.[14] A half decade later, the team's and Brandi's particular impact lingers. Soccer has emerged as the American girl's sport of choice, and five years later, for $439, one can still buy the famous

photo of Brandi on her knees (it made the cover of *Time* magazine),
framed in tandem with a hand-signed black Nike sports bra.

I have wondered if the image of jersey-throwing Brandi lingers because it is a picture of exuberant freedom—an American woman having gone for and triumphed in her pursuit of a global victory. In
throwing off the jersey, perhaps she also cast aside whatever doubts
she or anyone else might have harbored about her (or any woman's)
place in sports or the power of American women's sports to launch
millions into explosive celebration.

There's something about throwing it to the wind—be it a soccer
jersey, a graduation cap, Boston harbor tea, caution, or whatever—
that embodies freedom. And freedom is a consummate American
value. Think: Declaration of *Independence*. Think: Martin Luther King
Jr.'s "*Free* at last! *Free* at last! Thank God Almighty, we are *free* at last!"
Think: baseball games and rousing echoes of "the land of the *free* and
the home of the brave." Freedom is woven into the DNA of our
national identity.

As single American women, we possess this freedom like never before. The 1970s TV program *The Mary Tyler Moore Show* (still shown in
reruns) offered what for me was the first memorable image of this
freedom. The show's opening climaxed with Mary Richards, who was
employed at a TV newsroom and living in her own apartment, standing in downtown Minneapolis by a fountain, spontaneously throwing
her hat into the windy sky. The theme song declared, "You're gonna
make it after all!" At the time, it seemed revolutionary—a show about
a never-married woman in the workplace—but now, it's just reality.
Everywhere. I'm talking about women across political and religious
spectrums, about your twenty-eight-year-old single female Republi-
can; your thirty-three-year-old former college classmate teaching elementary school; your twenty-four-year-old youth group leader;
your thirty-seven-year-old cousin working as a mortgage broker in
New York or Miami or Phoenix; or perhaps even you.

Women today are free on so many levels, big and small. We are free, for example, to dress the way we want. Just yesterday I ran into the grocery store to get some half-and-half. Walking by me were two teenage girls, strolling along in baggy jeans, long-sleeved plaid shirts, and hijabs (head scarves). It dawned on me how strange it is that I can bop around in Lycra (I had just worked out) or a hijab—I am free to don, or not don, almost any article of clothing I'd like without thinking twice.

Freedom extends to other, more significant arenas as well. We are free to buy a home anywhere we can afford one; to campaign or vote or not vote for whomever; to commit or not; to marry or not; to do just about anything we desire. These are freedoms far beyond what my grandmother knew.

Sitting alone on my back porch with my half-and-half laden coffee, I realize that all this freedom can make a girl a little heady. Says Søren Kierkegaard, a nineteenth-century Danish philosopher, "Anxiety is the dizziness of freedom." It's funny, that anxiety thing. Though I don't believe it's unique to single American women, anxiety does seem to show up, often quietly, in the lives of many of my friends, and not just the ones who are tortured poetess types. I think of one friend in Denver who talks about the deep-breathing exercises she does to conquer it. Another in Seattle talks about needing "lots of time to process." Still another friend in Richmond talks about coming home to her very cute house and her lovable dogs and nevertheless encountering a strange sense of unidentifiable uneasiness.

Anxiety has crept over me along the way as well. I remember walking along the sidewalk one morning on my way to a job that I could do reasonably well but didn't like. As I contemplated the myriad of vocational options available, suddenly some unnamed angst shot through me. Technically free to move, travel, work, play, and sleep anywhere, I found and sometimes still find that my very surroundings can almost lose solidity. It's like I'm suddenly walking on water, and in response I do the most natural thing possible: I begin to sink.

Anxiety does seem linked at least in part to this endless freedom. A number of years ago, my friend Scoot and I leaned against the bumper of his Camry as we watched yet another friend drive away in the truck we'd loaded with all her goods. Scoot was twenty-seven and I was twenty-eight. We looked at each other in disbelief: How many friends would we have to watch disappear in the quest of another (good) opportunity? Even in relatively small Williamsburg, Virginia, where we lived, transience was the name of the game, and with each friend's departure—including, eventually, my own and then Scoot's—some strand in the fabric of each of our lives was pulled out. The widespread freedom to go wherever, whenever, can leave a woman a little less grounded.

It's not just the freedom for geographic or vocational transience, however, that can foster a low-grade anxiety. More significantly, it's the freedom from virtually all boundaries, at least relative to previous generations, that can leave a single woman reeling inside. Of course gravity, the stock market, and others' driving habits do limit us. But so many other boundaries have been busted. Nobody is expected to believe that anything is absolutely, at all times, universally true; sex of any shape and size between any shaped or sized consenting adults is considered cool; what matters most is how one feels, and that can effortlessly shift with a bonus paycheck or an obnoxious driver.

Kierkegaard is right: All this unbounded freedom can leave a girl a little dizzy. Upon what do I base decisions about the future? How important is my job? What should I look for in a relationship? Can I really know anything for certain?

So . . . great. We're left with Mary Tyler Moore (aka Mary Richards) freely throwing her hat to the wind only to find herself splashing around in the nearby pool of existential angst. And Minneapolis gets cold in the winter. What, then, will enable Mary, or you or me, not just to hop out of the pool and dry off, but to really, freely, make it after all? It's a valid question.

Robert Frost, that early twentieth-century American poet, wrote, "You have freedom when you're easy in your harness." The man has a point. Boundaries and lines can be helpful. I read once about a study where children were allowed to play in a backyard that bumped up against undeveloped land. Ironically, with all that land available to tromp through, the children played close to the back stoop. But when a fence was erected, the children moved away from the back stoop, running and playing freely within the new limits. Though it might seem counterintuitive, in actuality, the fence created more freedom.

So, while we're not seven-year-old children, I cannot help but wonder if the same principle of limits bringing freedom is at work in our adult lives. I've seen it in my own. Predictably, the harness-freedom connection first hit home in my relationships with men.

Thinking about the freedom thing, I began carefully observing how I related to men. To my chagrin, I discovered that in my seemingly footloose and fancy-free search for a mate, I wasn't actually free at all. Rather, I was quietly bound by criteria such as "Is this guy a potential trophy husband?" or "Is this evening fulfilling me?" Clearly, the first question is not a fundamental consideration for lifelong intimacy and compatibility. And the latter question—while worth asking in some form—when it's first and foremost on my mind, distorts my lens, making the entire interaction about me. That's a death trap! Honestly, *enslaved* might be the best word, because in practice, large parts of me were serving these criteria. The criteria had, if you will, mastered me—and not for my own good.

There's some strange paradox at work: A woman can be technically free—bound by little external constraint—and still not be free. It took me a while, then, to arrive at the point when I finally sat on my bedroom floor and risked a private experiment. I asked God, in a whisper, if he might teach me how to relate freely but on his terms with men. It was a hopeful and hesitant prayer—hesitant because there lurked the possibility that God's parameters might reshape me into a Stepford wife or a lonely nun; hopeful because Insta-Perma-Perfect-Man might appear on my doorstep the next morning.

Neither vision occurred. However, in inviting God's harness and direction (and the "how God leads" thing is another book in itself), I've noticed how I've been led onto more solid relational ground with men. It's not all about me anymore, and I'm even learning how to desire the best for the men I go out with, be they a trophy or a booby prize!

It would be wrong, however, to think that these "pseudo-freedom equals slavery" or "divine harness equals freedom" correlations are only true in relationships with men. There are so many places in my gut where I've been hooked by stupid or hard things. Room with me, work on a team with me, sit in the classroom in which I taught, date me, ride shotgun in my car, be a member of my family, or read my journal. If you bothered to look, you'd see lots of chains weighing me down. Utterly free to roam the globe, I can still be bound by chains of hurt, insecurity, impatience, mistrust, lies, and fear (to name a few!).

But lest the scenario sound too bleak, I've begun to find some freedom in these areas too. Sometimes it has come through those same whispered prayers inviting a challenge to my freewheeling autonomy: "Help me, please." Other times, it has come in reading words like those of the apostle Paul, who wrote: "You . . . are controlled not by the sinful nature but by the Spirit, if the Spirit of God lives in you."[15]

One winter when I was in graduate school, I spent a January term in Jackson, Mississippi, working at a biracial ministry among the poor, Voice of Calvary. As I later wrote in a newsletter for VOC, "When I first arrived here, on a barely conscious level, I realized I had associated black men with rape and black women with 'help.'" That's ugly. And it's wrong. But you know what, though I'd never been taught those things—intellectually I found such thoughts abhorrent—some place hidden in my soul held such thoughts captive. There was something in me that was, as I was not-so-flatteringly called by a colleague in his book, "a Waspy white know-it-all."[16] Ooh . . . ouch!

How amazing, then, Paul's words were to me when I realized I could say to God, "I am wrong, I am sorry, change me." And then to know that his Spirit really does enable me to freely believe and function out of what is true—that all people are created, equally, in God's image—how wonderful is that? How good it is to be able to live more and more in what is true. That is real freedom.

The net result (from a far longer story than I've made it) has not been perfect-perspective, hook-free, or miraculously mapped living in any area of my life. And like with the men thing, in the race arena my steps have been small, helped by many patient African-American friends who've cared enough to see me live from truth. But like the children in the fenced backyard, as I acknowledge the lines of reality that God has drawn—around relationships and race and many other things—I find myself far less enslaved to the back porch, or to the murky shadows of my own heart. I live with greater abandon.

David, a king of Israel, summed up the experience well when he wrote, "The boundary lines have fallen for me in pleasant places; surely I have a delightful inheritance. I will praise the LORD, who counsels me; even at night my heart instructs me."[17] He seemed to really get the connection between God's counsel in our hearts, the benefit of boundaries, and the ensuing sense of delight.

Freedom is amazing. Living in twenty-first-century America as college-educated single women, we have—thanks to many who went before us—so many freedoms. Some are small and humorous. One friend reminds me that she can go online and instantly pull up the names and mini-profiles of more than two hundred men in her zip code area who are interested in dating someone! Some are more significant. A Turkish acquaintance of mine speaks of the freedom she has in this country, unlike in her country of origin, to carve her own way, regardless of the social standing of her family. Some are evolving. One African-American girlfriend of mine says that though she lives chronically aware of the racial injustice in this country, in the day-to-day, she feels far safer than her foremothers did. God knows, literally, that all these freedoms, from the puny to the profound to those in process, are good gifts.

In searching for real freedom, I've found this irony—like that image of the World Cup jersey-throw—lingering everywhere. It's this: The capacity to walk bravely and freely in this land of the free and the brave—regardless of where you come from or how you got here—apparently stems from following God's lead. Nobody talks about this. After all, freedom seems like it should be simply the absence of restraint. But that's not enough. With busted boundaries galore, so many of my friends—women and men—still yearn for some elusive sense of freedom. Maybe more than ever before, walking bravely and freely demands the constraint of a heart aligned with True North, because the cultural maps are now so up for grabs.

Regardless, I know that when a few of my friends and I have risked deferring to an ultimate harness and ceased chafing at the bit, strange new sensations of freedom have been aroused. It smacks of that ease Robert Frost discussed. And in another strange, ironic twist, that sensation in turn propels us toward valuing the bigger, large-scale freedoms we enjoy.

Have you ever watched seagulls at the beach? Cruising the skies, they seem to own the place, having the time of their lives. They appear to be some of the freest creatures alive. They've thrown not just their hats or jerseys to the wind, but their very selves. Watch, though, a lone seagull anxiously committed to disregarding the strong land breezes that try to blow him out to sea. Poor gull. He struggles, he labors, he might even eat the sand fiddler he is trying to swoop down upon. But he is far from free. This is because, as Tim Keller, a minister in New York City, points out, birds are really only free to the degree they are flying within the limits of the air currents. We can't necessarily see those currents, but we can tell when the birds sail with them.

Wouldn't it be fascinating to get together a few of your friends—Mary Richards, Brandi Chastain, Martin Luther King Jr., Robert Frost, King David, and the rest? We could throw out the topic of "freedom" and see where the conversation takes us. That's a great thing about this country: We can talk about anything. But my guess is, if we all talked long and honestly enough, we would conclude something that the birds already seem to know. Birds don't get dizzy in their freedom because, simply, they are upheld, propelled, and aligned with the wind.

CHAPTER 8

Not Gettin' It

For three years in Washington, DC, I rode the metro to work. On Friday afternoons at about 5:45, I'd emerge from underground to hear the voice of "the Flower Man" melodiously shouting, "Get your roses, five dollars; two for eight!" The Flower Man was cute: six feet three, blond hair, big smile kind of cute. And for about five months of Fridays we made that wry, brief kind of eye contact that goes along with that kind of cute.

Then one Saturday, who showed up on the public tennis court next to me but the Flower Man? He did look cute in tennis clothes. Eventually, we got to talking and he took my number. Turns out the Flower Man (aka Chris) rented a house not too far from mine, one I typically passed on my power walks. From our brief conversation I could tell we were pretty different people (him selling flowers to pedestrians, me selling international public policy think tank projects to large founda-

tions; him hoping one day to complete college, me having done the
graduate school thing ten years before; him loving above all to "party
with the boys," me wanting above all else a boy to love me), but I was
glad for the chance meeting. Every Friday after that, I found myself
walking home with one or two sets of beautiful (free) roses, some
compliments in my pocket, and a little twinkle in my eye.

Weeks later, one warm evening, I just happened, more or less, to be
power walking by the Flower Man's house while he was in his driveway working on his truck. He commented about how good I looked
in my walking shorts and joked, "Hey, why don't we get married?" I
said, smiling wryly, "It's a possibility, but I'd have to get to know you
first." Eventually, as the conversation and chemistry continued to
bubble, I found myself wanting to risk revealing a little more about
myself. I talked about my upcoming vocational switch into "ministry,"
which of course begged a few more questions and comments. "Yep,
Chris," I replied, "I'm a Christian." I felt nervous saying it because of all
the stereotypes that accompany that label. Plus, it revealed more of
my heart than had anything in our six months of playful flirting, and I
had no idea how he'd respond. But I figured it was worth the risk.
Who could predict what would happen? We did have chemistry.

He paused for a minute and then said, "Ah, that's okay. I know what
that means; it means if we go out, you won't sleep with me on the first
few dates. That's cool."

"Well," I responded, somewhat taken aback, "uh, that's not exactly
what it means. I mean, it does mean that. But it means a little more as
well." I wish I'd had a more brilliant, incisive, alluringly faith-building
response, but I didn't. The conversation quickly switched topics to
bands and clubs or something in that vein, and I eventually continued
power walking. Chris, the Flower Man, never called me. And though
our Friday friendship continued to grow in a flirtatious, salesman/client,
counselor/counselee fashion (becoming almost brother/sister-esque),
the only other mention of us as a potential "us" came three years later. I

ran into him outside a coffee place near the metro, and he bemoaned, "Ah, Connally, why won't you go out with me? Is it because you know that I just want you for your body?" In three years I'd grown up a lot and could now laugh. "Yep, Chris, it's because I know you just want me for my body. Believe me, I'm flattered, but I need a little more!" He laughed too and hopped into his truck to drive on.

∝

Sex. It makes the world go round. Literally. If it weren't for sex, the population would dry up. But as a single woman who believes—as crazy at it sounds—that sex was designed to be experienced solely within marriage, I don't worry about the population drying up. Rather, I worry that I might. One of my living nightmares is that I'll wake up one day, shriveled, living with a bunch of cats, rocking in a chair, wearing a beige cardigan sweater—a completely asexual, withered old maid. I think I read a short story about such a woman when I was in high school—probably written by someone just like that—and the image has stayed lodged in my brain. One time I mentioned this to my (then) boss, and he burst out laughing. "Connally, you don't need to worry about that. Even if you never married, you wouldn't turn out to be a shriveled-up old maid. Plus, aren't you allergic to cats?" Very funny. And easy for him to say—the father of eight kids.

Nope, being celibate stinks. There's no way around it—around the stinky part, that is. There is a way around celibacy. I remember watching a postmortem special on John F. Kennedy Jr. with two long-time girlfriends. He had been such a handsome man. Sitting in the living room, watching that show, I was filled with this ache to be with such a handsome man. I exclaimed to my friends, "Agh, sometimes I just want to have sex so badly I could explode!" One, a mother of two, laughed and smiled. The other looked me in the eye. "Connally, you are a grown woman. You can have sex! No one is stopping you."

Suddenly I felt my oddity. It was weird to be thirty-five and not having sex—at least it seemed very weird. Had I lived in another century, I might have been a grandmother by this age. Had I lived in another century, however, I might not have been so inundated with images of sex, sex, sex everywhere. But I'm living now, in a sex-saturated culture, and every movie poster, every beer, car, soft drink, or cigarette ad, and every song on the radio seem to remind me of my celibacy. Even when it's not some promotion of illicit, mechanistic, consumer copulation, something else—October's bright blue sky, May's silken breezes, or a man's gentle listening—can stir in me a longing to connect. Perhaps this is a longing for eternity, as some have suggested (actually, there's much truth worth unpacking in that thought), but on some level, it is simply a desire for warm flesh to touch warm flesh.

So, how does one handle living a life devoid of warm flesh touching warm flesh? I've encountered just about as many answers to this question as I have people. One friend said very candidly that he genuinely worried about people who were not having sex. I'll never forget it. We were eating Thai food and he said, "Yep. I think either you 'get it' or you get weird." That felt like a dagger. Here I am, as my limited consolation for celibacy, thinking that I'm doing well holding on to something good, and instead, I feel for an instant like I'm incubating a disease! A girlfriend said she thought it was best for people to go ahead and sleep together, that such a complete sexual expression had more integrity than all the "in-between, stopping and starting" of her technically virginal friends who had pseudo-sex with lots of people. Pseudo-sex, she said—and I did agree with this—just bred ambiguity and weirdness.

One day when I was teaching high school English (fifth period—I shall never forget that class), I was in a particularly foul mood. Truly, that class could have put a twenty-five-year master teacher in a foul mood, but it was particularly torturous for me, a twenty-five-year-old brand-new teacher. I do not remember the exact sequence of events, but I know it culminated with a kid I'll call Jimmy (greasy, longish blond hair; in tenth grade for the second year; wearing tight, skinny jeans) standing up and yelling: "I know what Miss Gilliam's problem is—she ain't gettin' any!" Amazingly, the class went absolutely silent—something they never did. His words shocked even them, and Misty—a tough cookie in her own right but one who had slowly come over to my side—said, "Shut up, Jimmy. Sit down."

I took one moment to assess the situation and decided Misty's words, still echoing, were enough, and I moved forward as if nothing had happened. Jimmy and I would talk later. We went on with *Julius Caesar*. Funny thing is, the rest of the day, I couldn't help but wonder, *Is Jimmy right? Maybe that is my problem. I ain't gettin' any!*

As I write, I realize how many of my experiences have related to the novelty and even absurdity of my seemingly self-imposed (but divinely sustained, I'm convinced) celibacy. One time while I was in grad school, after an evening of waiting tables, I was hanging out with a few other waiters and waitresses. Per usual, the conversation went to sex, and I tried to throw in a few contributing words—something to the effect of God designing it, it being a good thing, etc. Suddenly, someone declared aloud, "Wait a minute, are you saying you don't have sex?" You would have thought I had said that I murdered my mother. Glasses stopped clinking. Cigarettes were put down. All eyes turned toward me. "Uh, yep, I guess that's what I'm saying."

To be considered absurd or odd is no great privilege. But the harder part for me has been feeling like I'm missing out on this ultimate human experience that the whole world around me relishes daily. A friend of mine once said that the idol of single celibates is sex. I think he is right, though for many of my female friends, the idol includes more than just a physical act. But regardless of the gender nuances, how then is a single woman supposed to view, feel, and think about sexual intimacy when, in fact, she ain't gettin' any? How does she kill off her idols without vilifying sexual desire and becoming dried up? Or, put another way, how does she hold on to her God-given yearnings without becoming a slave to her desire for a husband? Frankly, I don't know. I think at some level there's simply an element of relentless struggle in this arena for someone who doesn't feel sexually shut down but is practicing celibacy. One seminary student I knew who was by all contemporary standards very "hot" explained to me that as he saw it, everyone who was celibate by obedience (versus personal preference) got a taste of sharing in the sufferings of Christ. As Jason understood the New Testament, Jesus was anxiously longing for the day when his bride—all his followers from all of history, aka the church—would one day be fully with him. That not-yet-met ache for union with his bride, Jason said to me, was an aspect of Jesus' ongoing suffering with which we could identify. Actually, he made sense. Still, while knowing Jesus suffers with me helps temper the sting, it doesn't fully eradicate it. And in a culture accustomed to numbing life's pain with sex as the chief narcotic, it's a double whammy.

Some suggest temporary fixes like pouring your energy into working on your stuff, getting "marriageable," meeting people, etc. Undoubtedly good things, they still don't solve the problem. I started to read one book about dumping the whole dating paradigm and working with a "courtship" framework, but the examples and experiences of the author seemed so far removed from my experience that I never got past chapter one.[18] Once I asked a group of slightly older women with whom I was in a regular study group, "So, what do you guys do with sexual energy when there is no outlet?" Somebody squeaked out something about aerobics while everyone else looked down at the floor. Ironically, I felt the same oddity I'd felt that night in the bar—as if I'd just confessed some strange, mortifying secret!

As I've listened to friends and to myself struggle with this question, "What do I do with my sexual desire?" the most encouraging answer—if not new, at least reframed—came from a woman named

Lilian Calles Barger, to whom I had confessed my fear of ending up withered, asexual, and cat-hoarding (no offense to my numerous friends who love their cats). She told me I didn't need to fear drying up because actually, what keeps a person alive as a sexual being is giving of him- or herself. It's not what someone is *not getting* that matters; it's what he or she is *giving*.

Her words flipped on a light for me. I then remembered words I'd read in Ronald Rolheiser's book *The Holy Longing: The Search for a Christian Spirituality*:

> Spirituality concerns what we do with desire. It takes its root in the eros inside of us and it is all about how we shape and discipline that eros. . . . We think of [Mother Teresa] . . . as a spiritual woman. Yet she was a very erotic woman, . . . because she was a dynamo of energy . . . poured out for God and the poor.[19]

Mother Teresa got wrinkled, but she didn't dry up. And the reason, I'm coming to see, is just as Lilian said: She kept giving of herself.

Now mind you, I have no desire to be a nun. I visited Mother Teresa's convent in Calcutta. It was an island of beauty and rest in a sea of smoggy, ratty poverty, but it spawned in me no desire to join. However, I couldn't deny the burst of life I received in that short time from watching and briefly experiencing those women giving up their lives for others. Pete, an acquaintance of mine who has labored with questions of singleness and sexual desire, believes that so much of the angst among singles in our culture is that we've framed every aspect of life in terms of consumerism. Relationships, particularly including issues of sexuality, are framed in terms of "getting," not giving. That, he contends, breeds selfishness at the core. And with selfishness at the core, all of us, even the most sexually active, dry up.

There have been moments, such as a particularly languid summer night at the beach or the evening after a long weekend of speaking, when my heart and body feel a longing for some greater connection, some greater release; a part of me suddenly aches to curl up with my man, to have warm flesh touch warm flesh. Sitting in that unfulfilled moment, there is an undeniable ache, almost physical in nature. I used to fear that ache—that if left unfulfilled, it would make me crazy or barren or a social misfit. But I don't fear the ache anymore. Yes, it feels bad, but I know that in the end, the ache does not have to destroy me. Rather, I have slowly been discovering that the disease to be feared is not—contrary to so many of the voices that surround me—*not gettin' it*, but rather, it's *not givin' it*. So my hope has become that I will grow in my capacity to give it, give myself—whether that takes the form of my body, my heart, my time, my energy, my mind, or my dreams—in ways that give life to others. Because at the end of the day—regardless of how achy and bad or luxuriously beautiful that day has been—giving it is what ultimately matters.

CHAPTER 9

Gettin' It

Putting down a draft of the previous chapter, my friend raised her eyebrows, pursed her lips, and asked, "But what do you say to the women who *are* getting it?" It's a good question, but the truth is, my vision and vocabulary for discussions with my friends who *are* getting it has had to grow slowly. As you might guess from the "Not Gettin' It" chapter, I came of age in a slightly split context in terms of sex.

My church culture, which was soulful and incisive in many ways, got strangely hush-hush around the topic of sex. It was an unspoken given that sex outside of marriage was a no-no, though once I did hear a minister talk about the problems with "petting" (it gets your body revved up with nowhere to go). But who ever used the word *petting* anyhow? (Even today, such language makes me cringe.) Meanwhile, steeped in sex ed since fifth grade, I was quite familiar with talk of body parts, birth control, etc. Plus, as I moved through my teens into my twenties, many of my friends seemed increasingly tapped into some illicit fun line that was directly linked to sex, so it was never far from our thoughts. I'll never forget my second year in college when one roommate responded to another roommate's question, "What's your favorite exercise?" With a bold and wide grin, she declared: "Sex!" Somehow the word "tennis" never made it off my lips.

Since college, however, I've had to find words—in large measure because I have needed language to make sense of my own experience, as well as to be able to communicate meaningfully with many of my friends. A few years ago, a group of women and I sat in a friend's apartment, each sharing our "sex journeys." That sounds a bit bizarre, but it was actually an honest attempt to understand each of our backgrounds as we explored together what some of the writers in both the Old and New Testaments said about sex. How were you raised? What have your experiences been? What do you believe is true or real in terms of sex now? Why have you come to that conclusion? Answers to the questions varied. Two women referenced the historical perspective of their mothers (sex only in marriage) but said they were glad they'd gone beyond that. Most of the women came out in what I've realized is a fairly typical place: Casual sex with random guys is no good; sex within the context of any committed relationship is fine.

I began my story in about fifth or sixth grade, when my friends and I started talking about "bases." Fourth base, of course, was a home run—going all the way. Bases one to three were the steps from here to there. It was clear early on (probably because of church and my mother) that fourth base was off-limits. But as I moved into high school, I discovered a lot of fuzziness of opinion about bases one to three. Honestly, it began to seem almost un-American to not be making it to the other bases at some point. After all, on the TV classic *Happy Days*, wasn't the Fonz always tumbling around with women in the backseat of the steamed-up Chevy?

It wasn't until my late twenties that I began to realize that my accumulated tumblings had created strange emotional ties to certain men who had long since fallen out of my life. At first I paid no attention to these memories—shoving them into the "youthful and normal experimentation" category. But no sooner did I shove them in, they'd bust out again. These weren't just vague memories; rather, specific images would come back, grab hold, and magnify in my imagination. I'd be left with a feeling of unidentifiable guilt (after all, I'd never broken the fourth-base rule, so what was the problem?), as well as feelings of hollow dissatisfaction and a stirred-up sexual appetite. Like a recurring viral cold sore on my lip, these memories would pop up out of nowhere, particularly when I was tired or lonely, and they'd prompt a self-consciousness that would draw me inward, hampering my engagement with people and with God.

Now that all sounds a little heavy and dark—and I certainly don't regret every kiss. Actually, the loss of the joy of "light romantic interplay," as one friend calls it, is a sad fallout of a culture obsessed with sex and orgasm. But in a strange way, some of my memories haunted and served as a strong wake-up call. They galvanized my attention to the effects physical connections with men have on my heart. This was attention I'd previously preferred not to pay. Actually, most people I know don't pay much attention to their hearts. One of my dear friends, referring to a group of her girlfriends with whom we had just watched *Sex and the City*, commented, "Okay, maybe that show's over the top. But most of my friends do sleep around, and they aren't bothered by any regret. It's just fun for them; it's not that big a deal."

I don't know if the unbothered part was actually true or just talk. I suspect that it's possible, over time, to pay so little attention to your own heart that nothing bothers you. Joanne, a thirtysomething friend, admits sensing herself grow "inured, dulled, or anesthetized to [her] own heart" as she moved through sexual encounters, even though they were with men she seriously dated and cared for. But late at night or over a cup of coffee on a back porch somewhere, when

friends and I get vulnerable and drop our masks, we acknowledge that
sexual connections with men—which don't just occur sliding into
home plate—have shocking and residual potency. At the risk of
sounding like somebody's mother, or now perhaps grandmother:
Randomly tumbling around in the backseat with the Fonz or on the
mattress with your boyfriend can have powerful consequences.

Sex is a powerful thing. On one hand, looking around our culture,
this seems obvious. Sex sells. Look at car commercials or Victoria's
Secret ads. Just link your product to sex, and that product will inevitably harness the powerful, relentless energy of sex. And yet, at the
same time, the "power piece" isn't all that clear because sex—bases
one to four and the rest of the field—is chronically trivialized. Look
at those same ads: Sex also appears to be simply a random, popular
tool to wield at will, to get what you want (customers, kicks, connections, kudos, whatever). The cultural messages are schizo-
phrenic: Sex is a fun toy, a water pistol, available in neon colors,
from the small handheld to the super soaker! And, sex is nuclear energy, an explosively powerful and desirable fission that can move
mountains. We are left to make our way between these two contra-
dictory visions—sex as part water gun, part nuclear reactor—piec-
ing together inadequate philosophies that generally suit our most
recent desires.

But regardless of our particular philosophies, sex seems to have its
own real and relentless power. It's decidedly closer to nuclear energy
(which can flatten as well as move mountains) than a squirt of water.
For instance, have you ever known (or been) someone who stayed
hooked in a relationship because of the physical connection? One
friend of mine, Page—who harbored no evident taboos about sex outside of marriage—admitted that she stayed with Clarke far too long
because, as she saw in retrospect, their potent sexual fusion blurred
her perspective. The fact that he was intellectually ambivalent about
(and probably emotionally incapable of) marriage—something she

wanted—was lost in the swirling energy of jazzed-up hormones and genuine moments of oneness.

Actually, according to therapist Paula Rinehart in her book *Sex and the Soul of a Woman*, that hormone-induced, almost-blinding intoxication is one of the big points of sex. Referring to studies of newlyweds in the first eighteen months of marriage, whose oxytocin levels fly off the charts (oxytocin is the hormone that makes people feel close and intimate), she writes, "Every physical aspect of their being conspires to bring them together and to give them great pleasure in the process." This "romance cocktail," she writes, shows "how invested God is in bringing a man and a woman together,"[20] an investment that can keep them bonded even in the shaky or dark times.

It's that power thing again. As casual as I (or most of the white noise of songs, movies, and happy hour chatter) might like to make it, sexual connection in all its permutations is far more loaded than we know. Not only does it deeply bond people, but it also has the power to reshape—even heal, under the right circumstances—a person's soul. Paula goes on to write about the molten quality of a woman's heart during sex. When a woman is that vulnerable and there's a man there "who has pledged himself to her, come what may—something broken, deeper than words can touch, [can be] healed, piece by tiny piece."[21] And, as a therapist who has seen and counseled hundreds of women, she concludes: "All the therapy on the planet cannot accomplish what the arms of the man you love can."[22]

No wonder, then, that we want to get it! No wonder Page wanted to keep getting it with Clarke. Who wouldn't? Bonding, healing, pleasure? In an isolating and fragmenting world, those things sound really, really good. Plus, if you really can get it for the cost of a squirt gun . . .

But then there's that *pledge* thing, that newly*wed* thing. Paula's perspective presumes sexual bonding within the context of marriage. This, she points out, is because that's how God designed it. The per-

manent exclusivity of God's profoundly intimate and life-giving relationship with his people is to be fleshed out in the permanent
exclusivity of an intimate and life-giving relationship between a man
and a woman.* And this fleshing out isn't just to make God more evident, though it does that. Actually, it's what's best for people, too. If
sex is this super-mega bonding agent, then gluing together and ripping apart, one time or many, in isolation or in bulk, can only do damage (try it sometime with Elmer's and construction paper). Hence the
old "What God has joined together, let no man put asunder" marriage
proclamation.

When my friend Page finally broke up with Clarke, it was really
hard on her. If what Paula and the Scriptures say is true, it makes
sense: The sundering severed something in her that wasn't designed
to be severed, and it was painful. I read an article once in the editorial
section of the *Washington Post*. Patricia Dalton, a DC psychologist,
came at things from a different vantage point than Paula's faith-based
one, but interestingly, she came to the same conclusion. "I am convinced," she wrote, "that breakups are much harder when unmarried
couples have had sex to bring them closer. That's what sex is supposed to do, after all, in evolutionary terms: promote pair bonding
and thereby provide a secure environment for raising offspring."[23] The
bottom line seems to be the same: Broken sexual bonds do damage.

Of course, as I write this, I am conscious that I have friends who are
sleeping around with no glaring consequences. And two of the
women from the discussion group I mentioned at the outset are happily married to the men they previously lived with—they claim it was
a bonding that didn't result in a painful separation. To all of this I say,
"Thank God for his gracious gifts." I don't begrudge anyone a happy
ending—which comes as a gift, not necessarily as a reward for particular behavior. And though another couple admitted to me that their

*See the biblical book of Hosea, as well as Paul's letter to the Ephesians (5:22-33).

premarriage sexual encounters spawned trust issues after they were married (if the *lack* of marriage wasn't a factor in their or their spouse's decision to sleep with someone, why would the *presence* of marriage be a factor?), I have dear friends with different views. They wonder if my perspective is simply a result of some hang-up. Perhaps I got stuck in some nineteenth-century loophole?

My thinking *is* strange thinking, in the sense of being oddly out of place these days. This idea of sexual connection* being saved for the marriage bed does sound incredibly *out there* in many, many, many circles—Christian or not. One of my former roommates, Dolly, was once in a quiet conversation at a funeral reception, where the discussion turned to marriage and sex. A woman in the group slowly deduced Dolly's perspective and then declared at the top of her lungs, "A virgin? Dolly's a virgin? I don't think I've ever met one!" The already quiet room got suddenly silent. Dead silent. Then the chuckles began. Dolly, a confident, sexy lady in her own right, was suddenly the talk of the funeral!

In a different vein, but equally revealing of the perceived strangeness of celibacy, is another friend's experience. She has no particular moral convictions about sex in terms of marriage but has slept with only three men in her life. One was her on-again, off-again boyfriend of ten years, and since then, two others. As a result, her (I think wellmeaning) friends have repeatedly tried to explain to her that her problem in life—why she doesn't currently have a boyfriend—is her frigidity. It's ironic, as she looks far from frigid. But it is a foreign concept to her friends and her that maybe something inside her is naturally, intuitively, and rightly recoiling from the prospect of bonding and separating, bonding and separating. Her heart is pushing back, even if she has no language to explain beyond, "I don't know, I'm just not that into it."

---

*For practical purposes, I'm calling anything that brings either person to orgasm sexual connection.

Recently, my friend Gwen from Philadelphia has helped me to get some words around questions of sexuality and the heart. In her volunteer work with single women, she has heard much about their sexual experiences. Women from a Christian background, Gwen says, don't necessarily look terribly different from other women. While "waiting for the right guy" is a familiar phrase, the "right guy" often turns out to be any guy "who pays attention to a woman whose soul is starving for attention [which so many of us *are* in a busy, transient, intimacy-starved culture]. And, of course, if he fits, say, 40 to 50 percent of the qualifications to be a potential life partner, then sex is right." A woman's reasoning can go something like this: "I waited until I was out of college. I'm a professional now. I can make this choice for myself. This might be the one I've been waiting for, and after all, the potential I see in him is great." In short, if a woman wants to know intimacy and love, this seems like the most direct way.

Gwen suspects that for many women, regardless of faith background, sexual experience can seem like the only *real* way to know intimacy and love. Our culture emphasizes knowing by experiencing versus knowing by believing. *I can only know, and thereby trust, that which I can touch.* So it's not a big leap to think that the only way we can know intimacy and love with another person is to *experience* him or her. And what could be a more fully knowledge-giving experience than sexual connection? As Joanne, whom I mentioned earlier, says, "If you are taking off your clothes and going inside one another's bodies, what else can you do to better know somebody?" And if I want to *know* that I'm not alone, or *know* that I am healthy, or *know* that I am alive, what could give me that knowledge more than the real, undeniable, tangible experience of sex and its potential power to bond, heal, and please?

Speaking of *please*, please don't get me wrong. I love sensory experience and am completely convinced that it is one of the valid ways God has given us to know him and one another. I love bodies touch-

ing bodies! Actually, one time after I realized that full sexual experience wasn't going to be around any immediate corner for me, I
remember praying, "God, then help me be as fully and sensuously
alive as possible, as is!"* I don't think it's in anyone's prayer book, but I
meant it from my hair follicles to my toenails. I agree with another
friend who begged me not to vilify light romantic interplay:

> It would be a shame for a woman who really loves God to
> allow fear and a holier-than-thou purity to separate her from
> the possibility of enjoying physical affection. It's just sad
> when people become paranoid and can't be free to express
> themselves through kissing and hugging and holding hands
> and enjoying romance. Just don't call the good dirty.

I don't want to call the good dirty. But what I've seen as I've begun
paying attention to my own heart and listening to those who are paying attention to theirs is what my friend Gwen has seen: In a culture
without boundaries, acceptable talk about sexual limits often focuses
on issues of health and safety. And issues of health and safety are reduced to discussions about condoms and birth control. But what
about the health and safety of a woman's heart and soul? Aren't they
worth paying attention to?

When I finally began paying attention to mine, I saw that accompanying much of my physical interaction with men was an undercurrent of damaging selfishness and idolatry in my heart. I don't mean
that I overtly worshipped any guy (okay, with one possible exception) or that I consciously set out to use anyone (though I'm not above

*This can also raise the question of masturbation (i.e., what to do with your sexual desire
when there are no right avenues for sexual expression). While there's much debate around
this, I'll only say that while I don't think masturbation is the end of the world or some
kind of sin, it does seem to be taking one's sexuality completely into one's own hands, so
to speak. And though it can offer physical relief, it's a poor substitute for a relationship
and can sometimes leave a woman more dissatisfied.

that). Rather, like most women, I've wanted loving, restful intimacy—
to know and be known. It's just that I've wanted it on my own terms,
within my reach.

At certain moments, it has seemed to be within reach. I could feel a
power at work (I think every honest woman recognizes that in certain
situations, women have a power that can bring men to their knees).
Somehow, I wanted to exercise that sexual power not just for personal
pleasure, but also in the misplaced hope that in so doing, experiencing a guy in this way would touch me, fill me, love me, rescue me. I
wanted this mysterious connection with this mini-god to save the lost
parts of me.

Much of this longing felt so close to what Paula was talking about
in terms of bonding and healing, but I realize now that it was only a
shadow of the real thing. It was not a gift I was contentedly and gratefully receiving from a trustworthy God on his terms (which is what
sex is designed to be). Rather, it was an idol I was trying to create and
clutch tightly with my own hands, for my own purposes. So close,
and yet so far.

There is some mystery as to why God's context seems to matter.
Nevertheless, there is something about the mutual, permanent marriage commitment—God's frame or structure—that seems to qualita-
tively change the nature of sexual connection. Commitment seems to
ground sexual connection in something real. Somehow, real things
like poor health or bad breath, experienced in the context of a no-
holds-barred commitment, taste better than kisses tainted by the air
of fleeting experimentation. It does make sense: The soothing ham-
mock that holds two people in a warm embrace is great when it is well
grounded but dangerous when it slips from its supports.

"Did God really say, 'You must not eat from any tree in the garden'?" the wily serpent asked the woman.

She replied, "We may eat fruit from the trees in the garden, but

God did say, 'You must not eat fruit from the tree that is in the middle of the garden, and you must not touch it, or you will die.'"

"You will not surely die," the serpent said to the woman.

"When the woman saw that the fruit of the tree was good . . . pleasing . . . and desirable . . . she took some and ate it." [24]

So goes the infamous tale of Eve and the wily serpent. How strangely relevant it is—her confrontation with a choice not dissimilar to the choices that face so many of my friends and me. Let's face it, God was asking her to know and do—or not do—something because he said it. "Trust me," says God. "My reasons are good." Whoa, that just doesn't fly so well today. Meanwhile, the serpent offered a far more tangible, sensory experience. "Eat it," he said. "Your reasons are good." So Eve, like all of us (in so many areas including but not limited to sexuality), had a choice. In what, or whom, would she trust?

Maybe that question would be my response to the original question at hand in this chapter. "What do you say to the women who *are* getting it?" My best response is, "In whom or in what will you trust?" I don't say that flippantly. Trusting, for me, is a struggle.

But maybe before you answer that question, I'd simply suggest two things: First, try paying honest and loving attention to your own heart. Sometimes the little pangs that are so easy to ignore are trying to speak volumes of truth. Maybe there's a good reason that, like my friend, at the end of the day, you're just not that into it. Or maybe, like many of us, relationship endings have left your heart torn asunder. Or maybe, like me, you know there's some faint smell of selfishness involved in your physical relationships that you'd rather just ignore. It's not easy to pay attention, but it's never too late. And how great it is to have a heart that is growing more secure, forgiven, free.

Second, risk paying attention to God's heart. In searching for a vision and vocabulary for sex, I've discovered that God isn't a killjoy. Bonding, healing, and pleasure are his ideas. We—I—do not need to try to sneak them past God in hopes of getting good things from homemade gods because the real God is tightfisted. Instead, as we learn to go to the Creator, we can ask him to lay those gifts on us. If he chooses to use marriage and sex as one of his means, great. But if not (and way into my thirties now, I know that there are no guarantees), it's worth the risk to trust that he'll come through via other means. The bonds, healing, and pleasures I've found outside of sexual connection and outside of marriage are very real. I can see that God's fingerprints are everywhere in my life: in my family, my friendships, my vocation, and a thousand little piddly places. All of life, not just sex, is charged with his glory.

As the creator not of water guns, but of waterfalls; not of nuclear reactors, but the sun itself, God has the power to deliver love and life to all of us, including the currently single and celibate types. Honestly, I don't always feel it, and sometimes like Eve I want a serious bite of that fruit now, on my terms. But I'm starting to believe that when the time is right, God can deliver more fruit than I could ever want. As a matter of fact, he's got the power to bring the orchard straight to me! After all, for him, moving mountains is mere child's play.

CHAPTER 10

Girls Loving Girls

My sister-in-law Chantal and I decided it was time to leave the family behind and go for a walk down the beach, just to catch up. Sporting our sunglasses and black "illusion" bathing suits, we began our walk. A few minutes into the walk in a burst of enthusiasm, Chantal reached over, grabbed my hand, tucked my arm under hers, and leaned her head on my arm (I'm about eight inches taller). For Chantal, ethnically Lebanese, hugs and hand-holding are as much a part of her blood as flat bread and strong coffee, but as she did it, I instantly became aware of how weird we might appear: sunglassed women walking down the beach, holding hands. In a flash, before I could even stop myself, I thought, *I hope people don't think we're gay!*

Bothered that the thought had even come into my mind, I just kept walking with her, choosing to enjoy the warmth and affection that this sweet sister-in-love (as my family refers to my brothers' wives) had to offer. I couldn't shake being bothered, though. Reflecting on it later that day, I realized that I was both saddened and angered that the thought had even entered my mind. I was saddened because I grew up in a touchy-feely family—a family for whom back rubs, kisses, hair tousling, and long hugs were just givens. None of it was self-consciously intentional, none of it was remotely sexualized, and all of it was simply part of the rhythm of our interaction. But somehow, that previously assumed wall of protection surrounding the expression of innocent affection and healthy friendships between women had been breeched in my imagination. I felt angry.

I have talked about this with a number of my girlfriends, and across the board, there seems to be an increasing self-consciousness about all kinds of affection between women. One friend, a nurse, said she watched her interactions with other women particularly because, lacking a boyfriend, she didn't want to risk appearing like a "lipstick lesbian." That, she explained, was a woman who did not externally fit a more "butch" stereotype but still "liked girls."

Recently, I had a conversation with a woman who is a wife, mother, grandmother, and college professor. As we chatted, she said she had seen in college-age women a greatly heightened sensitivity to the question of sexual identity, one which she said would have never crossed her mind in her college days, forty-plus years ago. She talked about how her best friend from college was a "dear," a friend to whom she would pour out her heart, and to whom she would gush about her love for her. They had sometimes slept in the same bed and pledged lifelong friendship. None of it ever had a sexual dimension, even in their imaginations. Now, she said, she feels almost embarrassed to talk about it in front of younger women because to their ears it sounds so *iffy*.

Her words about her friendship seemed to echo something I observed as I read *Divine Secrets of the Ya-Ya Sisterhood*. The four girls who comprise the sisterhood have a constant, loving affection that is often physical but never sexualized. Rather, their hugs and kisses are simply one type of bond among many that keep them connected to one another—a means for expressing joy in raucous good times and support in painful seasons. Actually, though the characters are different, I find in the Ya-Ya girls an echo of the females in my own family during holiday gatherings. Amid cooking binges, someone will inevitably feed another whose hands are busy a buttery taste of this or that food morsel, and at night, fatigued, we'll rub each other's feet or backs. It's not that these expressions of affection intentionally exclude men (the males always want in on the back rubs, if not the cooking); rather, it simply has always been a means of female bonding that nourishes each of us along the way.

I don't really know, then, what has happened to the wall protecting that kind of unself-conscious physical and emotional affection. Has it been knocked down by a hypersexualized culture that attributes an erotic motive to every motion? Was this wall also hiding a darker side to women's affection and therefore needed to come down? Could it be a little bit of both? The first chink in the wall for me came the summer after my first year in college, when I was a counselor at a girls' summer camp. I'd been at the camp for many summers and loved it: seemingly endless weeks replete with silly songs, macramé, cold lake swimming, and weekly dances with neighboring boys' camps.

One evening before taps, I was talking to the head counselor, nicknamed Blue, whom I had been bugging to show me a picture of the boyfriend whose letters arrived daily. Finally, in a moment of candor, she said, "I can't show you a picture of *him* because *he's* a *she*." Thinking she was kidding, I laughed. "Ha-ha. Very funny!" When her face stayed straight, I swallowed hard, decided Jesus wanted me to stay in the room, and eventually stammered out something to the effect of, "Well, Blue, I still love you." She then filled me in on all the other people at camp over the years who had experimented with homosexuality. I was dumbfounded. It's not that I was a total innocent, but as she named people, I remember wrinkling my forehead, trying to reframe things, and not knowing what to do with my new pictures.

In the almost twenty years since that time, I have encountered friends whose perspectives on girls loving girls have covered the spectrum. One friend, Ro, who was openly gay, expressed her amazement that I, someone she considered "generally loving and open-minded" could see a problem with this. She concluded that my "repressive religious heritage" had warped my thinking. Other friends have struggled with emotional dependence; many are confused about what's healthy and what's not in their desires for emotional connection with girlfriends. Conversely, one friend, Kay, told me she'd never even thought about the things I'd written about in this chapter. "I've got my issues," she commented, "but confusion about my girlfriends has never been one of them!" Another friend explained that an uncle's abuse had left her trusting women far more easily, while yet another mentioned a fearfulness about getting too close to other women because of potential emotional complications. "Men are just easier to be friends with; they aren't as complex as we are, so there's no weirdness." Of course, some take it all less seriously. "Oh, maybe it would be easier if we lived in a man-free world!" laughingly declared one friend, whose boyfriend had called her controlling because she wanted marriage and children. But regardless of any of our perspectives, it seems everyone knows that the public landscape of possibilities has changed.

I know that once the walls protecting and defining innocent and healthy affection have fallen in a culture, they are hard to rebuild. This is especially true when many do not want the walls that used to prohibit same-sex sexual expression rebuilt. I think of a popular movie from a few years ago, *The Hours*. Incredibly well acted, it sent the quiet sideline message that sexual ambiguity between women can be a given—between sisters or friends, in this century or another—and ultimately, lesbianism is just another option—at least as long as you choose it from your heart. I disagree with this message, and I know to some, that makes me a killjoy who wants to dictate what's right and wrong in sexual expression. Backed into a corner, eventually I fall back on the teachings of the Old and New Testaments, but those only carry weight with certain people.

Still, even with that one line drawn, not every question is answered. What is a girl to do when it comes to loving other girls well? Reluctantly, I am thinking that naïveté as an option must go. Some guiding image of "Shirley Temple meets the Ya-Ya sisterhood" isn't a strong enough picture to define or protect female friendships in this era. The competition is just too strong. Think of Victoria's Secret catalogs filled with images of *woman as predator*. Scary. Or there's the almost hip mystique that same-sex sexual experimentation can take on. One high school girl explained to me that at her boarding school, all the cool girls were "bi." Throw on top of that a culture that is intimacy deprived, and the potential for real confusion is obvious. Even when the questions aren't overtly sexual in nature, there's much discussion about enmeshment and boundaries in friendships. Clearly, the walls have come down, and a lot of us are wondering how to proceed. Somehow, a way has to be consciously reforged—within the realities of a real, twenty-first-century, hypersexualized and intimacy-starved culture—for girls to love girls well.

I can't, in one short chapter, fully address questions of healthy female friendships (nor would I be able to, even given unlimited pages). This is one of those topics in which scholars get PhDs and about which counselors write long books. But in talking with many of my friends, and in taking a long hard look at my own life, I've seen a few common building blocks.

My friend Jen Ennis, who is a wise woman and a therapist to boot, said to me on the heels of one of our conversations, "Wow, it strikes me how vulnerable you are." She was not talking about my capacity to be "real" or "transparent." Rather, she meant that I have an *unprotected* feel about me, as if my basic yearnings for love, affection, intimacy, and belonging (all very normal and good desires) leave me susceptible to manipulation or seduction by those who do not have my best interests at heart. And in spite of the fact that I can navigate public transportation, fly around the world, handle my auto mechanic, balance my checkbook (more or less), and even prayerfully stare down—one time—a potential predator in a park, she was and is right. I do think I walk around unprotected.

But I don't think it's just me. I see this in many of my single girlfriends. Our longings to know and be known, to love and be loved, to belong and have others who belong to us—these very strengths (for that's what they are) can almost serve as liabilities in a world where anything goes. They can leave us too open to fall into a variety of traps, often including emotionally enmeshed—or even, in some cases, sexualized—friendships.

A number of years ago, I read an editorial about marriage by Meg Greenfield, at the time a writer for both *Newsweek* and the *Washington Post*. Marriage, she reasoned, is strained in our country not because it is valued too little but because it is valued too highly. We expect too much of it, she explained. The emotional needs and relational desires that were once met through both nuclear and extended families, which themselves were grounded in larger communities, are now telescoped onto only one relationship: that of husband/wife. That burden, she argued, creates a level of pressure that no marriage is intended to sustain. How much more so then, I have to wonder, does this apply to individual friendships—especially among single women?

Imagine a single woman, living away from her family in a professional world. Due to serial disappointments, busyness, fatigue, or simply a lack of candidates, her hope or even desire for marriage begins to wane. Or more dramatically, picture a woman who has suffered abuse by one or more men. She has been robbed of her capacity to envision healthy intimacy or family. Regardless of the severity of the scenario shaping a woman's heart, with no solid community to which she can belong and contribute—they're hard to come by in urban, transient settings—where will a woman go to meet her God-given need for love? She might start trying harder with men. She might pour more of herself into her work. Or, as I often see with single women, she might eventually default to her friendships with women, or perhaps one friendship in particular, for her soul's sole provision.

I began seeing signs of this in myself as I moved into my late twenties. The men in my life—a few of whom I was quite open to and desirous of—seemed so much less constant and reliable than the women. My roommates were there to hang out and eat dinner with; half the men I met would throw out a dinner invitation and then never call. My roommates and I would stay up late having meaningful conversations about life, our beliefs, and our dreams; many of the men I met—with some notable exceptions—not only had little language for these things, but little interest in gaining it. So I found myself relying more and more on my close friends.

On one hand, there was nothing wrong with this. Women have relied on one another for emotional support for aeons. But on the other hand, I felt new and strange flashes of jealousy, need, desire, and anger cropping up in disproportionate amounts in a few friendships. It was as if I was hooked by the potential of "connection" in friendships that in reality weren't designed to bear the kind of weight I hoped to put on them. I could not articulate this at the time, but I knew enough about health to know that this wasn't it.

Emotional dependence, says author Lori Rentzel, "occurs when the ongoing presence and nurturing of another is believed to be necessary for personal security."[25] Unhealthy dependence can be particularly seductive because it gives us the feeling that "we have at least one relationship that we can count on and that we belong to someone."[26] I can think of one friendship in which there was a painful break a few years after college, and the break hurt me deeply. Too deeply.

In retrospect, I genuinely loved and still love this friend, and her rejection of me at the time was a legitimate loss. But in fairness, there was also a shady side to my sadness. The pain was partly the result of having, on some level, worshipped my friend's life-giving intelligence, beauty, and depth. So losing a connection with her felt uncannily close to losing a connection with the Source of Life itself. Of course, I never would have said that, because I knew she wasn't God, but something in my heart had been leaning on her in this wrong way, giving her more emotional power in my life than was good for either of us. And I didn't know it until she pulled away.

Actually, that wake-up call helped me begin facing the fact that any relationship can get twisted. Moms and dads, heroes and feelings (like pleasure, intimacy, power, or comfort), or men and women—no one and no thing is immune from being put on the altar and wrongly worshipped. Gratefully, and probably as an expression of God's grace for my weakness, I've experienced the protective fences of a schedule filled with meaningful work, a sensitive conscience, husbands who've come along for my friends, a family to keep going back to, a relentless desire for a husband, the presence of a few older and wiser friends who've let me voice my loneliness and disappointments without shame, and a God who can simply fill up my soul with himself, supernaturally.

Still, especially when I'm feeling emotionally thirsty but busily swimming in a sea of salt water, I'm not immune to the feeling of an emotional "pull" to make people my savior. Conscious of it, I sometimes must simply choose to resist the pull. While, as one friend says, it's "much harder and not nearly as instantly gratifying to allow my needs to be met from a whole array of resources," it seems to be the strategy that is the most life-giving. I've got to believe that God will give me, today, my daily bread. And I've got to trust that, as another friend put it, such provision includes food for my heart.

Actually, another friend and I were just laughing today about neediness. Hers, she said, has been shrinking. "I've gone from being a

Hoover vacuum cleaner making that loud sucking sound to just being, well"—and picking up her soda, she sucked through the straw— "something like this." We both laughed. It's good when we can get our needs out in the light and laugh about them.

Nevertheless, the abundance of single (or single longer) women in our culture seems to create a climate ripe for emotional confusion. And without making a gigantic leap, it's not hard to imagine that in a society where sexual connection in any context, at any cost, has become a god—a false god that can wound hearts—emotional dependence, especially if it is lodged in connection with one friend, can sexualize among women. I've even seen this among those who decidedly believe that the sexualization of female friendships is wrong. Caroline, whom I mentioned in an earlier chapter, spoke candidly of her experience:

> I found that when I was in an emotionally dependent
> relationship with another woman, I slid down the slippery
> slope toward a sexualized friendship. I remember the intensity
> when we first started hanging out—the sensations reminded
> me of when I first started dating Theo. The desire to see her,
> and the sadness when I didn't. But I woke up in horror when I
> realized that at some point the hug of my friend and
> connecting with her literally sexually stimulated my body. I
> could not control it. It was one of the scariest things I have
> ever been through because it was so confusing. I knew it was
> wrong, but I had nowhere safe to go. I had no way out, and it
> felt so beyond my control. I did not know what to do. I have a
> good father; I have dated men; I have always wanted men. [So
> this] caught me totally off guard—if this could hook me, it
> could hook anyone. But nobody ever talks about lesbianism in
> my circles. It's completely taboo.

Yuck. So much of this has a heavy, shadowy feel. It makes me not even want to talk about it. But I can't escape the notion that naming the truth, bringing it out into the light, is a key to reforging a path for girls to love girls well. None of this mess shocks God—the darkness isn't dark to him. So while there's no need to dwell on every detail of what's shady, we don't need to fear getting slimed just because we talk candidly about the truth.

And sometimes the truth isn't slimy; it's just a valid struggle. I remember walking through bustling, downtown DC one day on my way to work. I'd come up from the metro, and tired just from thinking about the day ahead, I spotted this rather large, buxom, gray-haired grandmotherly lady walking slowly toward me. Such women are few and far between on rush-hour sidewalks. But there she was, and I found myself wanting to go up and just get a hug from her. I wanted to nestle down in her arms in a way that would comfort me in my anticipation of another cool, steely, and efficient workday. I was embarrassed that such a thought flashed through my mind. *Uh-oh, now you want to lay your head on the big, welcoming breast of a stranger? You're losing it, girl!* But in retrospect, I realized that what my heart was telling me I needed was and is a good thing—a life laced with motherly love, given and received.

I once heard the term "mother deprivation." My mother and I love each other imperfectly, but dearly. Nevertheless, we don't live near one another, and living on my own in a town that's friendly but rarely embracing or nurturing, I sometimes feel moments of mother deprivation. In a left-brained world valuing productivity and measurable results, I often find myself yearning for deep emotional connection for my heart. But even with the endless resources of friends, family, mentors, and a few beloved little people woven into my life, I still don't always know how to satisfy that desire for connection. On this side of heaven, I'm often reminded by friends, total satisfaction will be elusive. They are right. But the yearning, at least for me, is real, and I can have little else besides compassion for those who ache for this same thing and get mixed up in the process.

Still, the truth is that emotional connection or intimacy with others (women, men, or little people), while a good and right desire, cannot be our ultimate god. That, as my father likes to say, "is the bottom line." I always thought that finding those people—men and women—with whom I clicked was the thing to shoot for. You know, that person you meet at a party with whom you could talk for hours. Or that friend whose answers to life's questions make complete sense to you. And while there's nothing wrong, and very much right, with finding friends with whom we share a sense of humor, enjoy time together, or dream about the future, when our affection becomes the center of our world—whether or not this affection slides into something sexual—it ruins everything.

Author and minister John Piper uses this metaphor: When God is not the center of our "planets of passion," when we make anyone or anything else the sun in our universe, so to speak—inevitably, our planets of passion will spin out of order.[27] Our understanding of and desire for connection can get twisted. Or, as C. S. Lewis puts it in his book *The Four Loves*:

> Affection produces happiness if—and only if—there is common sense and give and take and "decency." . . . There is no disguising the fact that this means goodness; patience, self-denial, humility, and *the continual intervention of a far higher sort of love than Affection*, in itself, can ever be. That is the whole point. If we try to live by Affection alone, Affection will "go bad on us."[28] *(emphasis added)*

Maybe all of this is why the first two of the Ten Commandments are these: "You shall have no other gods before me. You shall not make for yourself an idol in the form of anything in heaven above or on the earth beneath or in the waters below."[29] God wants to protect us from affection gone bad. And the antidote is to keep him, the Source of "a far higher sort of love," central in every single relationship, including our closest girlfriends.

That "continual . . . far higher sort of love" can only be the love that the triune God both puts into us and empowers us to share. I think in part because of pride and embarrassment, for a long time I didn't want to admit that I needed God's help in something as seemingly simple as friendships with other women. But gratefully, the truth caught up with me before too much damage had been done.

So how do we go forward? How do we "discover God's vision for relationships"?[30] I've found that the discovery process is closer to unearthing an archaeological site than it is to striking oil. Instead of God's vision bursting on the scene in one big, instant spurt, the picture normally emerges by unearthing that which has been buried, putting back together broken fragments, and accepting that the process is slow. Surrounding this entire discovery process, like a fence protecting the site, is one large, encompassing truth: With God's help, we must learn to relate not with the primary purpose of meeting our own needs, but as a friend of mine once heard Dr. Tim Keller say, as people "living for the redemption of the other."

For me, such living has begun with the acknowledgment of my capacity to do the opposite. Specifically, when I find myself wanting more from a friend than she wants to or should give, I admit it (to God and maybe another person). And when I have found myself feeling clingy or preoccupied by the friendship, I do a quick little inventory. More often than not, it's my problem—I've made her central to my happiness on some level—and I simply ask for God's forgiveness and his help to relate differently. There are a few friendships I have had to let go of altogether—or let them take their natural scaled-back course without trying to force them to provide the closeness I've desired. But oftentimes, relating differently has meant something as simple as learning that a friend's unavailability is not necessarily all about me. Maybe she's *supposed* to be doing other things with other folks, and that's not only okay, it's good.

Living for the well-being of others might also mean forgiving those who have wrongly needed or mistreated me. I remember one quasi-friend who said to me after I'd listened to her process her muck over a few dinners, "Oh, please don't think I'm using you just for a sounding board; I really like you too." Hmm. . . . I'd never actually *thought* I was being used. But in retrospect, that was what was happening, and when I finally saw it (for example, in her lack of communication with me once her crises had passed), I had to admit her affection was primarily about what she could get. Then I had to forgive her. (It also proved to be a ripe occasion for asking why it had taken me a while to notice her motives.)

However, beyond these two crucial if difficult steps of repentance or forgiveness—there are no better words to do these steps justice—comes the fun stuff. First off, how wonderful is it that there is a God to whom friendship matters? God spoke to Moses, the Old Testament leader and prophet—scribe of the Ten Commandments, as a matter of fact—as a man speaks to a friend.[31] And Jesus was himself called a "friend of sinners."[32] God is into friendship. So, though it can be a wee tad humbling, I say, let's ask God to teach us what it is to be good friends as women, to have healthy intimacy and affection—even in a hypersexualized, intimacy-starved society. Let's ask him what it is to relate to one another so that the weirdness diminishes and the beauty that God has planted in each woman multiplies. And then let's take risks. I am completely convinced he will honor this desire in our lives.

I meet with a group of women every Friday morning. For the longest time, I felt like the newcomer to the group, a bit of an outsider, but I plugged away nevertheless. Sustained in large part by the good coffee and warm beauty of my new friend Ann's home, I practiced being honest, letting things evolve at a natural pace, and taking risks when the time was right. After one gathering, I found myself at my computer the next day, composing this e-mail. The metaphor is a bit earthy, but I think it summed up, and sums up, something of the good that can be found in women's friendships when we keep the "higher sort of love" central.

> *Dear You All:*
>
> *I remember a friend of mine who for a while had systemic candida, a problem that apparently left her intestines covered with a coating of yeast (this is a bit gross). Anyhow, this coating limited the intake of nutrients from her food, depleting her of important vitamins, minerals, etc. She had to take this antifungal medicine and do some extra vitamin supplemental stuff to get healthy. During my years in DC, sometimes I've felt like I haven't gotten the nutrients my heart and soul crave. Perhaps this has been because the nutrients in this city are so diluted by everyone's busyness, self-sufficiency, or agendas. Or maybe the nutrients are fine and I have had some film over my heart that keeps the real love out. Perhaps it's my issue or disease, so to speak—systemic candida of the heart/soul. Who knows? Perhaps it has been some of both. Anyhow, yesterday as I was driving away, I thought, Wow, my soul feels nourished. I realized that that was because I'd just gathered with a group of women who, in spite of admitting to being ill-disciplined, disappointed, not fully present, confused by God's sovereignty, and relationally and financially challenged (oooh, we sound good collectively, don't we?), there's still a real desire among us to love God, be loved by him, and lovingly engage with others around us. That sounds sort of basic, and yet it really touched my heart. You guys are better than antifungal medicine and extra vitamins. The time together was real food to me.*

When girls love girls well—when living for "the redemption of the other" is our focus—the loud sucking sound in each of us diminishes, and instead something life-giving is exchanged. As a result, everyone grows a bit more full emotionally and more grateful for the good they experience—and can help cultivate—in one another. Putting it more poetically, C. S. Lewis wrote, "[Friendship] is the instrument by which God reveals to each the beauties of all the others. . . . They are, like all beauties, derived from Him, and then, in a good Friendship, increased by Him through the Friendship itself."[33]

What a joy it is when I can give a girlfriend a hug as we meet for dinner after a long week. What a treat it is to kiss my mom good-bye when I leave her presence. How glad I am that I can look my two dear girlfriends since middle school in the eyes and say, meaning it from my heart's center, "I love you guys so much." What a gift it is to tell any one of my girlfriends on a day when she looks good, "Girl, you look beautiful" or hear it in return. And what a privilege it is to have a friend put her arm around my shoulder when I'm crying or look me in the eye and say, "Give me a break!" when I'm over-the-top. It is even satisfying to be able to love friends well by blessing them in their absence or departure—to another town, another job, another home, a long-awaited marriage, or a different set of friends. In other words, when girls love girls well, it's simply a wonderful gift.

So while I might not stroll blithely down the streets of Washington, DC, holding my girlfriends' hands (with the possible exception of my sister-in-love), with God's help I'm not going to let wrecked relational fences and the sexual madness of our culture keep me huddled alone, away from friends. Instead, I want to be a girl whose heart is turned first to the Source of a love far higher than affection. Then, trusting that the Source is big and good enough to provide all the love I need—through whomever or whatever means he chooses—I want to gladly keep growing to love other girls well.

CHAPTER 11

If Mama Ain't Happy...

If Mama ain't happy, ain't nobody happy, or so goes the old adage. Mothers come in many shapes and sizes—and some have more pronounced opinions about their daughters' choices and aspirations than others—but based on an informal survey of my friends, about eight out of ten moms worry about their grown, single daughters. About six of those eight worry about when and whom their daughters will marry. And many of us suspect, sometimes gratefully or enviously, that some moms are just good at keeping their opinions to themselves.

Once when my mother seemed overly concerned about some man issue in my life, I mentioned it to my boss. A wise, older man, he chuckled. "That, Connally, is what mothers do. They can't rest until their daughters are happily nested. It's in their genes."

Recently I e-mailed thirty or so single girlfriends to get input from their experiences with the subject of "Mothers, Daughters, Men, and

Singleness." In the past when I've asked for help on certain issues, I've received random, piecemeal e-mails. This time, the responses flooded in: "This seems like an important chapter." "This has been a sore spot with me and my mom." "Oh, Connally—I have so much I could say on this topic." One friend, Lynn, accurately noted, "It would be funny to see the other comments people share . . . kind of like doing the outtake scenes on DVDs."

The stories were funny, fascinating, and sometimes infuriating. But I don't think that's a surprise. Fraught with complexity, mother-daughter relationships have always been a focal point of discussion. *My Mother/My Self* was a book I heard a lot about for a while—perhaps when I was young and it was topping a best-seller list. Or think of the comic strip *Cathy*. It has been around since the 1970s, getting much of its mileage from the mother-daughter issue. I even had a good friend from college who wrote her doctoral thesis on the themes of motherhood in literature. And now with women staying single longer than ever before, questions about how to relate to our moms regarding these issues of men and singleness have had more time to multiply.

What makes these relationships particularly vexing is that we seem wired to pay attention to what our moms think, feel, and do in the men arena, even after we hit that theoretically adult age of twenty-one. Writes one woman, "Mothers are their daughters' role model, their biological and emotional road map, the arbiter of all their relationships."[34] Whew! Even if she's just partially right, that's a lot of weight on the relationship, especially when so many of us are in this single no-man's-land longer than our mothers ever were. How can our moms be maps for roads they never traveled? One friend, Abby, puts the tension this way: "[My mom] has been such a good model. She's set me up to have a deep longing to be able to be what she is and was, and there's no way I can in many respects, as a single woman. So now that I'm living in a phase of life she never experienced—post-college unintentional singleness—I feel like she can't be a role model for me in the way I'd like her to be and she'd probably like to be. I guess in some senses it creates a bit of a distance between us."

I think Abby's right. It's a little tough on daughters, but it's also a little tough on moms. When it comes to the topic of their single daughters and men, most mothers struggle. To speak or not to speak, that must be their question. And their answers are varied. Musing over my friends' responses, I realized that my own mom is in a breadth of good company.

On one end is Cynthia's mom, who Cynthia says "has never once, not even slightly, applied pressure on me to meet guys, date, or get married. She has never even asked if I've been on dates recently." On the other end is Amy's mom, who when Amy simply goes on one date "wants to know his last name so she can see how my name would sound if I were to marry this person." And there are many in between—Karen's mom, who "never wants to pry," sounds a little like Silvie's mom, who gives a lot of freedom but "gently teases me and encourages me in a general sense to pursue relationships."

Michelle's mom, like many moms, is a little torn. Says Michelle, "My mom did not marry until she was almost thirty, so on the one hand, she has told me many times she doesn't feel pressure that I should marry. However, when my boyfriend and I were struggling, she basically expressed the opinion that it was my fault—I had too high expectations." She played the old "too picky" card. Another friend's mom—and this did have DVD outtake quality—"literally forced" my friend to sign up with CatholicSingles.com. (Apparently it had worked magic, i.e., an engagement ring, for someone else's daughter.) So my friend, a social worker, admittedly went for the passive-aggressive approach in response. "For my user name I chose 'mommademe' . . . to let her know that I really did not want to be doing this."

What do we want from our moms? I think there are few whose ideal is a completely disinterested mother. Even Cynthia one day blurted out to her parents: "Don't you two want grandkids!? . . . I [am] grateful you don't dog me about dating, marriage, etc., like some of my friends' parents, but it would make me feel cared for if you'd at least express a little interest in something so important to me." On the other hand, nobody seems to want a mom who, perhaps out of her desperation for a married daughter, "drills her daughter on the prospects and blames her lack of prospects on the fact that she doesn't wear lipstick." That's no good either. Another friend summed up her basic desire with these words: "I wish my mom would say that she's praying for someone for me and that I need to trust God with this."

A caring, calming mom. It seems like most of us single women, at our core, desire a mother who "gets" us, loves us, has faith in and for us, listens to us, and advises us only when asked—all without pressuring us or needing us to be anything other than who we are. And many have experienced some of these aspects in their moms. There are moms who do pray, give support, and trust their daughters' decisions. But no mom seems to get it all right, all the time. And my stints of service as babysitter, camp counselor, godmother, aunt, and mentor have taught me what an impossibly tall order perfect nurture is. So what do you do when your mom falls short of perfection in this area? When she's too hands-off or too hands-on or too torn between the two?

My mom and I sat in my older brother Tommy's bedroom. Tommy had married long ago and had three super little boys, and my younger brother had recently stepped on the marriage track as well. Now the rose between the two thorns was left alone. The single daughter. Mid-thirties. Yick. It was not a place devoid of family, friends, health, money, or meaning. But it was a place I had never hoped to find myself. Nor had my mom.

My mom looked uncomfortable sitting in an inherited and decidedly stiff rocking chair. I sat in a slightly squishier chair, tapping one foot on top of the other. I had that clutchy, suffocating feeling in my guts. I knew I had to say something. "Mom, you just need to let me go." Big pause. Much silence. Yick.

"But I've always thought about letting you go to *someone*, not to *nothing*. One dreams of her daughter leaving, but it's so she can cleave. Not just so you can leave, alone, end of story." More silence. The problem was, I agreed with her. She wasn't imposing some 1950s suburban sitcom sensibility on me. That leave-and-cleave vision was my vision too. And yet at thirty-four, with no Beaver Cleaver to marry, I could feel my mom's control, worry, and angst about me and my future oozing onto me, tripping me up. It was as if her desire for me to be married (which in both of our minds was too directly linked to dreams of happiness) had begun inserting itself into our conversations, shaping her responses to what I'd share, shaping my willingness to be real.

My mother, who had always seemed like my source of wisdom and truth, seemed to be losing perspective. Was the problem that *she* needed me to be married? Singleness is, traditionally, a bit of a social snafu. Maybe it reflected poorly on her. Perhaps it appeared that her daughter had issues with men. Maybe it looked like there was something wrong with her as a mom. Maybe she was just worried about me being alone. I didn't know what it was, but when it came to the subject of me and marriage, her reasoning seemed to grow fuzzy. And that compounded my own insecurities and increasing sense of fragility in this area. So, like kudzu covering trees along a Southern interstate, the web of suffocation began to creep over our relationship.

"Mom, you just need to let me go," I repeated.

"I know, I know," she said slowly, rocking.

Letting your mom be human can be tough. I'm okay, more or less, with my humanity. Still, perhaps due to some residual nineteenth-century Victorian vision, I somehow secretly believe that moms are to be bastions of perfect love and kindness; of apple pie, homemade cookies, cheerleading, and organization; and possibly even bringers home of bacon. It's weird to think of your mom—my mom—as, well, for lack of a better word, a sinner like the rest of us. How does one look at her mom and acknowledge, *You, like me, have your strengths, your weaknesses. You, like me, have your issues, your stuff?* How does one accord her mother the honor she is due when that "stuff" pains both of you?

Different friends along the way have given me advice. "Oh, that's her issue." Or, "Just don't tell your mom so much." Both are true to a degree. There is wisdom in using discretion about what we divulge. As someone who likes to process aloud, it's especially easy to inadvertently lead someone else—including my mom—down too many emotional rabbit trails. Perhaps I needed to learn to button my lips about first dates and thereby spare my mom the temptation to evaluate last names, so to speak. And of course, if one's mom is poisonous or always sucking the oxygen out of the relationship, sometimes a decided "keep quiet" or "keep distant" policy is best.* But my mom isn't toxic. To the contrary, except in this arena, she has always seemed like my wise soul sister. Perhaps that's why her stumbling while walking with me, her wanting-to-be-married-but-still-single daughter, tripped me up as well.

I once heard a speaker say that we are doomed to repeat the failures of our parents until we can finally forgive them. I can't remember the reasoning behind this, but it's not hard to imagine. There must be something about recognizing and naming, then choosing to forgive—and thereby be severed from—the offenses of others that frees us from their grip. Otherwise, like a tape replayed repeatedly, perhaps the offense gets stuck in our heads and we find ourselves singing that very same tune to others.

It's difficult to remember all the exact moments, comments, or incidents for which I needed to forgive my mother. But in large part it was

*A friend of mine sought solace from her mother after a particularly painful breakup, but her mother's response dumbfounded her. Referencing my friend's relationship with her best friend, her mom—apparently trying to be helpful—suggested, "Well, you and Anne have always gotten along so well and seem so close. Maybe you're a lesbian." My breathless friend was crushed; a significant line had been crossed, and my friend changed her policy with her mother after that. Sometimes strong boundaries need to be drawn and held.

simply for being imperfect, for not trusting God with my future, for putting too much stock in the absolute necessity of marriage, for wanting to control something that's not so easily controlled. I don't suppose it's a surprise that those are the very same things I've needed forgiveness for too. Regularly. Anyhow, with the help of God and a few wise friends, I did it. I didn't want to *need* to forgive her; I would have much preferred her to be perfect. But forgiving her put an ax to my portion of the kudzu. I was freed up to keep moving into the uncertain territory of hoping for a mate without being enslaved to the desire.

There was, however, a special bonus that showed up a bit later. When my mom said, "I know, I know" while sitting in that rocker, she meant it. She didn't necessarily know what to do about it, but she must have meant it, because slowly, over the next year or two, something shifted in her. It was subtle but palpable. She did her work with God, perhaps with one or two of her friends. She came to the conclusion that in letting me and the marriage question go, she wasn't letting me go to *nothingness*. Yes, she, her mother, and her grandmother had all married around age twenty-one. So her models for the single-and-thirty-something mother-daughter stage were sparse. But, in an act of faith, she let me go, entrusting me and my future to God. Her part of the kudzu root got the ax too.

Of course, if spiritual realities aren't actual realities, if they are simply myths to fill up our life holes, she was just playing mind games with herself. And she could have been giving me permission to turn into some medieval mystic nutcase or a wannabe nun—cleaving to Jesus as my imaginary husband for the journey. I suppose I secretly worried that about myself for a while. (I have a dear friend who is an agnostic. When she and I discuss my faith, I sometimes feel like I'm a seven-year-old with Jesus as my make-believe friend.) But I know that is not the case. Nope. I've been watching. I've seen my mother's and my own breathing grow easier. The oxygen has returned. There's even enough air to chuckle about these men things, recognizing each of our limits. Maybe our hope in God's provision of goodness—which may or may not be equated with a husband—has deepened.

I know my experience with my mom is just *my* experience. Some moms get the "I just need you to cry with me, not fix me" thing much sooner than other moms. Some learn to stop playing the "[fill in the blank] is your problem, daughter" card sooner than others. Some moms say more than others. Some moms trust their daughters' decisions more easily than others. Some moms pray harder than others for their daughters' mates and futures. Some moms are overwhelmed and do nothing. But looking at moms and the concurrent turmoil of dating and adult singleness, it seems—clichéd as it might sound—that most moms just want their daughters to be happy. And most moms—whether they mention it or not—like my boss said, really do have a hard time resting until their daughters' happiness resides in a cozy, chick-filled nest. Maybe it is in the mom gene, after all.

Perhaps, then, the way we honor our mothers as we're walking single (by desire or not) is to see our moms as clearly as possible and forgive them for their sin. Even moms from the best gene pools—like daughters—are plagued by their own shadows, with flaws and failures nipping at their heels, tripping them up. If it's not in the why-aren't-you-married arena, it's in another. And a mother's issues will inevitably ooze onto her daughter. But as we forgive (probably it's a lifelong activity), we are freed to keep moving forward, to receive whatever abundant or limited love is offered. We might even grow to smile, understanding that as God is with us, loving us into adulthood, sometimes it's okay that "Grown don't mean nothing to a mother. A child is a child. They get bigger, older, but grown? What's that supposed to mean? In [a mother's heart] it don't mean a thing."[35]

CHAPTER 12

Dads and Daughters

As I walked through the bookstore, the sale table caught my eye. On it were two copies of the same book, each with a big orange sticker: "Reduced! $5." The title read *Always Daddy's Girl: Understanding Your Father's Impact on Who You Are.* Instantly, something inside said, *Buy the books and get Dad to read through one with you.* The thought gave me a wave of anxiety, but there they were, two of them, five dollars apiece. I bought them.

Two weeks later I ventured home for a visit. With nausea swelling in my guts, I approached my father as he sat in the den watching the news. (My mom was out of town for the weekend.)

"Uh, Dad. How's it going?"

"Just fine, honey. How was your trip?"

"Fine. Fine." Pleasantries. Pleasantries. I'm silently praying my guts out. "Hey, Dad. Remember how you read through that book with

Robert that one summer he was home?" (My younger brother had made stabs at getting my father to track with him on issues of spiritual growth and development.) "Well, I was, well, wondering if you might be willing to read a book with me, to well, uh, well . . . you know, talk about it." It never ceases to amaze me how seemingly brilliant ideas can suddenly feel ridiculously irrelevant when I voice them.

"What book is it?"

"Um . . . *Always Daddy's Girl.* . . . It's about the influence fathers have on their daughters. I haven't read it. I don't know if it is any good or not." Shuffle. Shuffle. Disclaimer. Disclaimer.

"Well, okay, I'd be willing to do that."

"You would?" Now I was most certainly regretting having verbalized the idea. Throwing up seemed like a distinct possibility. "Okay, we can work out the details later. But, uh, here's the book." I put it on the chair-side table and sprinted toward the kitchen.

⸎

Women and their fathers. If there's a topic that seems to elicit more hemming and hawing, more shuffling and head scratching, I don't know what it is. When I solicited input for this chapter from a variety of women, I noticed something strange. When it came to talking about *mothers,* my friends had instant, if varied, opinions. But when it came to *dads,* a cloud of hesitation seemed to descend. More than one friend said, in effect, "Whoa, that's way too deep. I could never explain it." Perhaps this is particularly true for single women, whose fathers are often the strongest male presence (even when emotionally distant or physically absent) in their lives.

Actually, I almost didn't write this chapter until I realized that my father as a named figure was strangely absent from this book. That struck me as odd until I realized that somewhere along the way, I had worked really hard at our relationship, been at peace with the outcome, and wasn't currently compelled by any particular father-angst.

And truthfully, when things are going well in my family, or in my life, I find that I default to treating my father like many people treat God: He's there, he's appreciated, but he's not particularly focused upon except at special occasions, in a crisis, or in my case, during Sunday calls. He's the big, benevolent given in the sky—forming the backdrop of much of who I am and how I live, giving me a fundamental security, but not serving as my focal point. Actually, I think this is the way he—my dad, not God—likes it. While he wants to be taken care of in his old age (chocolate chip cookies and foot rubs please him tremendously), he doesn't want to be worshipped and he likes to see that I'm off living my own life well.

But our relationship hasn't always had this sense of rest, and my friends' experiences have also been all over the map. So I think it is worth exploring dads and daughters, especially adult, single ones. As one friend of mine, Samantha, puts it:

> I think a father's role in a daughter's life is never over—even after he dies. His ideas, beliefs, and thoughts—both spoken and unspoken—will always resonate in our heads [and hearts]. Whether or not I choose to agree or live my life according to his value system is within my control, by God's grace. And with God's strength and wisdom, I will make choices for my own life. But the space or negative space our dads put in our minds is a fact that we all must face and get comfortable with.

And Samantha, by her own admission, should know. "I've put a lot of thought (and counseling money) into the whole gig!"

Dad-daughter relationships come in all stripes. In responses from twenty or so single friends, plus in innumerable conversations with women over the years, I've seen evidence of endless diversity. Says Leihlyn, "My dad was a very warm and sensitive man, and I think that has helped me to not be afraid of men in terms of being hurt physically or emotionally." Or there's Kim, who says of her dad, "Our relationship is both close and volatile. We're very alike. When we clash, we clash full-on. But no one in my life can pick me up like he can. When he says, 'Hey baby,' I'm golden."

At another point on the spectrum is Mary Kate: "My dad raised his kids to worship his god: financial security and safety. To achieve these ends you must get a job with the federal government and avoid certain people and their neighborhoods." Or Sheila: "My dad always complimented me and affirmed me verbally but didn't know how to love the whole of me. He rarely acknowledged the deeper things of emotions and needs in my life, because he was totally ill-equipped to deal with them." And there are endless other assorted experiences: "My dad is really a great friend . . . but we disagree in really healthy ways." "We seemed to lose a connection after my parents divorced." "My father was solid—a good provider materially, and somewhat encouraging." "I'd say we definitely have a dysfunctional relationship." Or "I function pretty independently, but I have this peace or security that my dad is there."

You get the idea. There's no one single descriptor for father-daughter relationships.

But what I have seen is that my friends' stories center around one common concept: *the impact of expectations.* There are fathers' expectations for their daughters and, perhaps equally, if not more potent, daughters' expectations—which often tumble seamlessly out of deep longings—for their fathers. And both have an impact on a woman's soul and choices.

I often hear twenty- or thirtysomething men talk about feeling inadequate relative to their fathers' expectations, spoken or not. But my girlfriends mention little about not living up to their fathers' expectations. That's not to say that there aren't fathers whose daughters have disappointed them and daughters who feel this. And of course a father who actively abuses or abused his daughter is in an entirely different category. But generally, women I have interacted with seem to have picked up on either the presence of high and motivating expectations ("Deep down, I really believed him when he said I could do anything I wanted to") or the *lack* of verbalized expectations ("I have no memory of my dad ever telling me that I was pretty. I was never affirmed in my femininity. [So] I didn't grow up believing that I was pretty or could be chosen—for lack of a better word").

Undoubtedly, such positive expectations, or their absence, have incredible power. Kim, the one with the explosive relationship with her dad, spoke about this. "He always had big dreams for me; he told me I could be the first black president, and I've always believed him. And he told me repeatedly, 'Never settle for a man who is not your match.' But who is my equal? Externally, I'm not that special. But internally—none are ever good enough." A dad seems to wield a measure of authority that shapes his daughter's heart. It doesn't matter if he's sitting passively in a lounge chair watching TV in a different state or actively engaged in watching his daughter's piano recital. Whatever the father communicates directly or indirectly to his daughter as a girl, she seems to absorb as truth.

Not surprisingly, expectations flow two ways. And perhaps because fathers seem to have this intrinsic authority (which they're always wielding, consciously or not), there is great power in the unmet expectations of a daughter for her father. I think of one friend who grew up chronically disappointed by her father. "Every year he promised to take us to the circus, and you know what, I'm still waiting." It's obvious how such a pattern of letdowns can set up a woman for easy disappointment or protective skepticism in all her relationships. Or as another friend puts it, "My father's place in my heart and psyche has been a challenge because he was unfaithful to my mother and has since been unfaithful to my stepmom, whom I really like. The impact of his infidelity on me has been that I find it hard to trust men to be faithful to me."

Even in less dramatic cases, failed expectations are tough pills to swallow. "One thing I've realized recently is how little either of my parents invested in our spiritual growth. I think they may have expected 'osmosis' to do the trick, but they did little to encourage and develop a spiritual side of us—except for obligatory church attendance . . . even when it didn't mean anything." Or in the vein of what I've heard repeatedly, "My dad makes sure my car is up and running . . . but I deeply desire someone who connects with my heart in a way my father only rarely has and does. Still, I know that I am lucky to have the father I have, who loves me without a doubt, even if he is unable to love me the way that I think I desire or need to be loved."

I remember when my dad and I were out hiking one day. I was back from graduate school, trying to figure out the next steps in my life, and we had decided to go on a two-hour round-trip hike in the Blue Ridge Mountains. As we walked up the trail, talking—most likely about the stock market or job options or maybe the family—I remember wishing down in the center of my soul that my dad were a poet or a philosopher. Or maybe a counselor. That, I figured, would make him one of those dads who could really *connect* with his daughter. And I remember wishing that he were more of a leader, a man who would more readily lead his family through the difficult waters of emotional conflict. But as we walked, he in his old khaki pants (he likes khakis better than jeans) and me trying to pull off the "hot outdoorsy chick" look, it dawned on me. *Connally, that's just not who he is. Accept him.*

That, however, can take some time.

My dad has always been a genuinely good citizen. He has been an elder in the church, lightly involved in politics, a Rotarian, and on the board of several different organizations. It means a lot to him that he is a solid presence in the community. One friend's dad summed it up well. With his long, back-of-the-throat Southern drawl, Mr. Yates declared, "Connally, your fah-thah is a prince of a fellah." He was and is right. My father is a tall, handsome, winsome gentleman. But not in a sterile way. No, he was a dad who would set me on his lap after work, rub his five o'clock shadow on my cheek, and sing "Thank Heaven for Little Girls" while I grinned and giggled and tried to get away.

Nevertheless, I grew up longing for a certain kind of strength or presence in my life that I sensed was missing. This absence was confusing because my dad and I really did connect well, our senses of humor always jelling. Just his presence, with a few painful exceptions, has almost always made me smile. So I've tried to ask myself what I was after. After all, my father was *present;* he did not disappear for eight years like one friend's father. To the contrary, he showed up at my girls' JV basketball games (now, that is commitment!) and was always cutting grass, doing errands, washing dishes, and providing both food and hugs in wonderful abundance. In retrospect, I think I was simply aching for a sense of emotional safety that I felt I lacked. For what it's worth—sometimes it does help to see how one person has parsed her experience—I'll try to explain.

Born right before World War II, my dad grew up in a world where most people didn't think about engaging culture out of one's personal faith, let alone discussing one's own spiritual growth or private emotions (though, as a man with a tender heart, his emotions are readily evident to any onlooker, particularly when he interacts with his grandchildren). Honestly, I do not think he ever learned to speak that language. Rather, he came of age in a culture that assumed a level of consensus (the 1950s white South), presumed church attendance unless one was Jewish, and saw it as a given that each person who played by the rules, faithfully doing his or her duty to God, family, church, work, and community, would do well.

I, however, have come of age in a culture spawning postmodernity, where questions around truth, gender, race, and sexuality for example—not assumptions about consensus—have been the name of the game. Incredible diversity has characterized the backgrounds (familial, religious, and cultural) of the people around me from the get-go. Growing up in this culture flooded by a tidal wave of change, I always wanted (especially as a teenager and young adult) to feel the safety of my father's presence in the confusion of it all. I yearned for my dad to speak out of his personal experience and conviction about *why* God was real and *how* one clung to one's faith around those questions of truth or gender or race or sexuality, for example. I particularly yearned for this because in my limited experience, I discovered that holding tightly to any convictions might land one on the cultural sidelines. For me, that felt lonely. But as my dad had little language for the things of personal faith, it sometimes seemed as if I were on my own and he was simply sitting back on slightly higher ground. In the things I believed mattered most, I felt left to swim upstream on my own.

Perhaps this would not have been such a big deal if my faith background were different. I hail from a tradition that speaks often of men as the *spiritual leaders* in their families. I've never been exactly sure what that is supposed to mean (I'm sure many others could speak to this kind of question with far greater eloquence), but I think it did set me up—rightly or wrongly—to expect my father's gutsy presence in a myriad of spiritually confusing arenas. He, however, took it to mean being faithful to lovingly provide for his family the best that he could. Quite probably, we were simply looking at the same expectation from two different sides of a cultural chasm.

In any case, navigating the gap between what my dad has had to offer (which as a single woman I've paid attention to in a way I might not were there a husband in the picture) and what I've felt I needed has been more of an art than a science. Sometimes now my dad and I laugh that God gave me to him as his daughter. Ironically, my very capacity to stay in our periodic dialogue about these things comes from the fact that I fundamentally trust my father. His stable love has imbued me with the confidence to challenge him. But as I do, my pointing out these aches and gaps has forced him far deeper into the churning cultural waters than he ever would have chosen. I think we both know that when and if I ever marry, my dad will have some hard-earned tips to give the lucky guy!

One time I was talking with a dear friend, Cheryl, trying to understand more about this topic of unmet expectations. "Is it okay," I wondered aloud, "to expect from a dad something that breeds a sense of safety in your guts or guidance for your life? Is that somehow an enmeshed, lazy, or demanding thing? Is it okay for kids but not grown-ups? And then what if he can't meet those needs? Is it okay to be hurt and disappointed, or are such feelings a product of some kind of victim mentality that can easily characterize my generation?"

Cheryl, who is trained in counseling and serves as the vice president for human resources of a 3,500-person organization (and is herself single), struck me with her response. She spoke of God setting up families for children to get tastes of godly strength through godly fathers. Early on in life, when a girl's vulnerability is indisputable, she can learn that there's a "benevolent strength in the universe; one that enables her to rest and go off duty; a good strength on which she can depend." This, she continued, is the gift a father should give his daughter, because in essence, he is modeling the truth about who God is. The impact of this on a daughter is that as she tastes the strength of a man used for good and not for evil, she's freed up as an adult to offer herself and her gifts to others. She knows somewhere deep in her soul that ultimately she doesn't have to watch her own back. She is already covered.

The problem is, as Cheryl didn't have to remind me, we all mess it up so badly. If somehow we skip over (or are skipped over in) the parts of childhood or young womanhood when we need to taste good strength, the impact can be potent. Whether it's the power of strength misused or the absence of strength completely, we are handicapped in our trust of the real and benevolent strength of God.

For single women trying to negotiate the world of workplace demands and politics, car and home maintenance, relationships with men from all kinds of backgrounds, and life in a lot of uncharted territory, this has powerful ramifications. Not only am I potentially alone and somewhat vulnerable in daily life (though friends can and do fill a lot of those gaps), but when my friends can't be there, when my weaknesses creep up and shake my confidence in the middle of the night, or when I'm just flat-out in over my head, if I can't "know in my knower" the benevolent strength of God, what happens? It isn't pretty.

Of course, no parent—including the most ideal fantasy father—can fully protect a child. No parent (or adult single daughter) can do right 100 percent of the time, nor can anyone control what goes on outside his or her sphere of influence. Maybe the best our parents can do is walk with us—even as single adults—as we get hurt and disappointed, even by them.* And maybe as adult single daughters, we need to learn how to name and grieve our fathers' failings, forgive them, and move on. I'm not saying it's easy, just possible.

Diane encountered this head-on when, without a place to go between jobs, she went home to live with her parents for nine months. Her story encapsulates this idea so well.

> I suppose living at home with my folks since May is a bit unorthodox for a single thirty-five-year-old. I wish I could say that it's helped my relationship with my dad. I feel the emotional distance now as much as ever. He buried his heart as a child, and I've never experienced a dad who is fully alive and engaged with his heart. . . . I suppose that's not all that uncommon . . . but it's even more painful because we were

---

*Periodically, I've gotten tastes of what it is to walk with an imperfect dad who can't solve my pain but doesn't run away from it. During a hard time of transition when I was about thirty, with no real relationship on the horizon and no meaningful work lined up, I felt lost and scared. My dad said to me one afternoon, "You're lonely, aren't you?" I acknowledged that I was. "I know what it is to be lonely; it's part of being human," he said. That was all there was to that conversation, but in revealing his heart and naming our shared experience, it did more to strengten me than just about anything else in the world he could have said or done.

always taught that our family was the "ideal." But my dad
doesn't challenge my mom's controlling nature, and she
doesn't challenge his passivity. . . . [I think at root the problem
is that] I don't know him and he doesn't know me. I think that
I was angry about [his emotional distance] for a long time.
[But] this summer has brought a lot of understanding and
forgiveness toward my parents. I understand more about my
parents' childhoods than I ever did before, and I can see that
they did the best job as parents that they knew how. Not that
my unmet needs aren't legitimate, but at this point, I have to
run to Jesus to fill the empty places.

Expecting that benevolent strength to show up in ways we can
experience or know is a fair longing. Grieving its past or present absence is legitimate. Forgiving our dads for being limited in ways
that left (and might still leave) an impact is necessary. Accepting
that no fallen human being, of any description, can fill our hungry
hearts is essential. And sometimes, repenting for making our dads
god—i.e., expecting from them the perfect provision, protection,
and soul-level connection that only God can give—is the first step
to coming to peace with all this dad stuff. Actually, that act of
taking our dads (or moms or boyfriends or husbands or whomever)
off the altar is what can free us to "run to Jesus," as Diane put it, "to
fill the empty places." We really can taste healing and new strength,
way down at the core. Regardless of who our fathers are or are not,
we are not alone. Good strength for the journey can and does
show up.

Sometimes strength comes in the provision of other good men
around us. One friend of mine, whose father was kind but not super-
communicative and lived a few thousand miles away, found an older
male mentor who "fathered" her professionally and, periodically,
would speak boldly into her personal life. His expectation for her to

make that workplace whirl, as well as to end up married one day, kept a large chunk of her soul alive. Likewise, a number of women have spoken about friends' husbands being there for them as uncles or brothers of sorts (as my brothers live overseas, I've found myself seeking this more myself). And for my friends who truly have no father, no father substitute, nor any sense of "someone watching out for them" (I think of one friend who was orphaned young and who is alienated from her brother), I'm silenced before their courageous and sometimes excruciating discovery of a God who is real, who shows up, and who watches their backs. That's a strength no one I know wants to be forced to discover.

In reflecting on this topic of fathers, Abby, in her early twenties, mentioned that she wished her dad would take a more intentional role in her life. And then she wrote, "Hmmm . . . maybe I should talk to him about that." As I scanned her words, I nodded in agreement. Sometimes our dads don't give strength because we don't ask. Most men don't enter into fatherhood with an intrinsic understanding of how much influence they have in the life of a girl or young woman. But many, including my father, can learn. Of course, asking doesn't always work. Diane said she'd spoken with both of her parents, and nothing changed. She is brave, she has grieved, and she is letting it go. But sometimes a little change in father-daughter relationships is possible.

∽

At the outset of this chapter, I mentioned that my dad and I agreed to read that book together. We planned to read a few chapters at a time and meet monthly at a mall located halfway between us to eat dinner and discuss what we'd read. Talk about embracing a path of sustained awkwardness. Our conversations were generally (1) twenty-five minutes of talk about the stock market, his business ventures, news about my job, and possibly a love life update (bare minimum); (2) twenty minutes of eating with more of the same discussion; and (3) fifteen long minutes of coffee and book discussion. But I wouldn't have missed those awkward, earnest conversations for the life of me.

There is one encounter I'll never forget. We were discussing a chapter about a father's praise and its effect on his daughter. Apparently, what a father dwells on is what a daughter will learn to consider valuable. If he praises success, she'll pursue success. If he comments a lot on physical beauty, she'll believe that's most important. You get the idea. Anyhow, a few of the women in the chapter mentioned how this dynamic skewed their views of both themselves and what was genuinely valuable in life. My dad kicked off our conversation:

"So, some of these gals have issues with their fathers because of things in their pasts. You don't have any of those kinds of issues with me, do you?" It wasn't the best safety-building opener, but I was willing to take what I could get.

"Well, Dad, it did seem as if you spent a lot of time mentioning my weight when I was growing up—you know, if I was too pudgy or had gained a few extra. But you didn't actually ever comment much on my character or spiritual development."

He paused for a few minutes, looked into his coffee cup, and then looked away. "Well, honestly, I wasn't that worried about your character or spiritual development. Those things seemed fine. You know, I'm more of a big picture, laissez-faire guy. And if something isn't broken, I don't fix it." Another pause. "But, well, your weight, now that did vacillate some. And of course, I wanted you to look as beautiful as I know you are."

I smiled. That's hard to parry. What girl doesn't want to hear from her father that he thinks she's basically doing just fine, and give or take a few pounds, is beautiful to boot? I'll always be grateful for my father's free and ample praise of my beauty and performance. But I still needed to risk explaining what else I hoped to hear from him, and why.

"No, Dad, I can see that. But you need to understand it from my point of view—you know, like the book was saying. What a dad primarily talks about or praises is what she ends up thinking is most important. So if you talk only about my weight or looks, that's what I end up thinking is most valuable, even if that's not the case or what you really believe. Like I'm Barbie or something."

I went on to explain that I needed to hear that he *really* personally believed the things that the church in which he'd raised us emphasized: that giving one's life to God in every area of life, starting with one's heart, was truly the most important thing. I wanted to hear from his own lips that in his estimation, my soul was more important than my dress size.

"Okay," he replied, nodding and taking me seriously. "I think I can understand that. Well, anything else?"

I smile now as I write this. Though it seemed like it lasted two hours, that conversation was about fifteen minutes long. But it was something. And I was glad I'd managed, however falteringly, to ask my dad, out loud, to express care for my heart and soul and not just my mind or body. Why that was so hard, I'm not sure. Maybe it was offering the *most* vulnerable piece of me for benevolent strength. And what if he just wasn't into that? So, probably to both of our relief, we quickly reverted back to discussing the Redskins.

A few minutes later we left the restaurant and stood in the parking lot saying good-bye. My dad and I smiled at each other, hugged, and squeezing me gently, he commented, "You know I think you really have lost some weight. You feel thinner."

"Dad!" I exclaimed, like a teacher who has told a student fifteen times not to lean back in his chair. "What did we just talk about? Have you already forgotten?"

"Oh, oh, oh . . . right . . . yes, sorry!" Suddenly I realized this really did not come naturally to him. "And your character," he said, stepping back and looking at me with a big and earnest grin, "your character is really good too!" I couldn't help but grin back.

Sometimes I suspect that if I'd been raised in a world like my father's, I might not have yearned for that dad who guts it out in the muck of a complicated, conflicted, postmodern world with a strong sense of soulful and spiritual engagement. But probably there would have been something else. So while I've wanted him to be more of a practitioner coach for some of the tricky areas, I've also learned, like many of my friends, to make peace and be grateful for the strengths he does possess (loyalty, kindness, provision, affection, love, and relentless humor). And as for the inevitable gaps—dads are human journeyers as well—I want to keep learning what Paul of the New Testament learned. He wrote, "I have learned to be content whatever the circumstances. I know what it is to be in need, and I know what it is to have plenty. I have learned the secret of being content in any and every situation, whether well fed or hungry, whether living in plenty or in want. *I can do everything through him who gives me strength.*"[36]

Most of my friends and I want to enjoy all the good strength that men, including but not limited to fathers, can offer. Perhaps my singleness, combined with an unmet desire for marriage, has made me unusually aware of my longing for that good strength. But as I've sought it (and listened to stories of fellow seekers), I've found that no dad (or anyone else, including myself) will ever be enough. And at the end of the day, regardless of what impact our fathers have had on our lives—making it harder or easier to trust the heavenly Father—we are all responsible for the choices we make. Some dads make those choices easier; some dads make them harder. But ultimately, each woman decides before her heavenly Father, with his help, who she will become.

This discovery has led (and keeps leading) me to the next: God really can and does give strength for every context—be it a single, urban, transient, busy, sad, exuberant, or simply unexpected scene. And as that reality seeps more deeply into the achy, longing parts of my guts, something in me grows a bit more content. As a flawed but loving daughter, I can rest and go off duty, enjoying yummy, calorie-laden chocolate chip cookies with my flawed but loving father. And with a grin, I can venture with greater confidence into the swirling cultural waters in which so many of my friends and I swim.

CHAPTER 13

So, Why Aren't You Married?

During his middle school years, my older brother subscribed to a humorous cartoon periodical called *Mad Magazine*. It had a section titled "Snappy Answers to Stupid Questions."

"So," asks the policeman, "why did you wreck the car?"

"Uh . . ." replied the driver, "because I thought it would be so much fun to meet a nice police officer like you!"

Sarcasm is no excuse for wit, a twelfth grade English teacher reminded us with a posted notice behind her desk. However, sometimes it can play a very close second. And while "Why aren't you married?" isn't necessarily a stupid question, it sometimes can bamboozle the one asked, leaving that person fumbling for an answer, perhaps even a snappy one.

In the now fifteen-plus years since college, I've gotten the "Why aren't you married?" question or its cousin from a greater variety of

folks than one might ever have imagined. Hannah, a third grader at
the time, asked with the earnestness of her age, "Why don't you have
a husband and kids? Aren't you lonely without a family?" A homeless
woman with whom I was eating lunch asked between bites of her
pizza, "So why aren't you married? Don't wanna be, eh?" A big-
hearted, completely sincere member of a board for which I was the
note taker declared in wonder during our break time, "I'm amazed!
Why hasn't anyone snatched you up yet?!" It's a bit awkward to know
how to respond. Most memorable, however, were the words spoken
to me at a wedding reception. The mother of the groom (whose bride
was four years my senior) took my then twenty-nine-year-old hands
in hers, looked directly in my eyes, and implored, "Why isn't a beautiful young woman like you married?"

At that moment, her words felt something like a plea for me to stop
doing or being something wrong, or maybe a prayer to God Almighty
on my behalf. In truth, I think it was a well-meant compliment flow-
ing out of motherly love. I remember looking her back in the eye with
the least vacant look I could conjure up and pleasantly mumbling
something about not having met the right person yet. A few hours
later, however, as her words still throbbed with their unintended
sting, I came up with my own snappy answer: "Well, see, actually, one
of my personalities, Jane to be precise, is married. But the other three,
well, Mary has too many issues; Sue is a commitment-phobe; and
Sally, well, she's just too independent!"

My twelfth grade English teacher was right, however. Sarcasm isn't
a wit substitute. And in the end, even the most deliciously crafted,
snappy response can't hold at bay a question that seems to nip the
heels of many single women as they move into their late twenties or
early thirties. *Yeah, why,* so many of my friends have wondered, *am I not
married?*

It's a question that more women than ever before are bumping up
against. In the last forty years, the population of twenty- to thirty-

something, college-educated, single women has exploded. In 1960 this group represented 1.6 percent of all women between the ages of twenty-five and thirty-four, or the rough equivalent of the then population of Fort Wayne, Indiana. Today, this percentage has grown to a staggering 28 percent, roughly equivalent to 2.3 million women or four Bostons.[37] So a lot of those four-Boston residents, scattered throughout the nation, are sitting around with their girlfriends, doing dinner on Friday nights, and drinking cups of coffee on Saturday mornings poking and prodding for answers to this same question about men and marriage.

In one sense, answers are out there. Actually, many people who ask the question already have answers in mind. Mary, my homeless friend, immediately attributed my singleness to a lack of desire. And the board member answered his own question with a rhetorical "No guy has been good enough yet?" I'm not sure if he meant that objectively or was implying something about my subjective judgment. For I have been told by numerous folks that perhaps I'm too *something*. The blank has been filled in with "picky," "eager," "real," "scared," and "threatening." I suppose all of those things probably have some grain of truth. My very down-to-earth hairstylist, Jackie, once commented, lowering and pointing her shears like a therapist with reading glasses, "Look. You're really into the God thing. If you're gonna find a man, he's gotta be into the God thing too. Cuz no guy is gonna want to compete with God."

Dr. Jackie was insightful. Maybe the "God thing" *has* gotten in the way.

Ironically, by the time I graduated from college, I had my own back-of-the-mind explanation for unmarried women over thirty. With nuns and wealthy heiresses as possible exceptions, the reasons seemed clear: Those women were either unusually unattractive, had issues with their fathers, or were gay. Where my conclusions came from, I'm not exactly sure. But you can imagine why I felt derailed when, as I neared the end of my twenty-ninth year, that dear woman held my hands and asked me why I wasn't married. What was I really going to say? "I'm not sure, but I guess it must be because I am ugly, have issues with my dad, or am gay."

I don't think any of this back-of-the-mind thinking is atypical. Libby, a single, forty-year-old friend, laughingly recounted a recent conversation with a twenty-one-year-old male friend of hers. (Note: Libby has modeled, is straight, and has normal father issues.) When she was talking with this young college guy about the recent engagement of a mutual twenty-something friend, the guy declared with a smile of knowing authority, "Well, Libby, it was inevitable that Kristen would get engaged; she's so great!" Of course, the message that he didn't even hear himself sending to Libby was clear: If A equals B (great women like Kristen inevitably get engaged), then unfortunately, "Not B" equals "Not A." In other words, unmarried women—such as Libby—must be lacking greatness.

It seems that no matter where you turn—to a third grader, a homeless woman, an esteemed and gifted board member, a college guy, a nurturing mother-type, or perhaps even yourself, the answer to the question "Why aren't you married?" often boils down to the same thing: It's probably your issue. Now occasionally some wise older married man will shake his head, roll his eyes, and offer with an exasperated sigh, "What's wrong with guys today? You are such a catch. They're all idiots." Or as a loving girlfriend once said to Libby, "You know, I have a beef with God about his not bringing you a husband!" In other words, the locus of responsibility does sometimes shift away from the single woman and her perhaps unidentifiable flaw.

As an aside, I've often wondered if straight, attractive, single women with an unfulfilled desire for marriage scare people. I told one friend that a weekend spent as the only unmarried bridesmaid in a wedding felt something akin to being plopped down naked with my upper-leg cellulite and stomach rolls on public display. Sure, everyone has some fat they wish would melt away, but mine was impossible to hide. And the sight seemed to cause a quizzical, slightly disturbed shock among otherwise gracious people. Picture crinkled noses, furrowed brows, and awkward silences. Perhaps straight, attractive, single women with an unfulfilled desire for marriage are an awkward reminder that all is not right with the world. And that's a bit of a conversation killer at a wedding.

Of course, some women do not want to get married. One friend of mine said candidly, "As I grew up, I could never see myself married. I had too many other things I wanted to do and be about." Fair enough. When asked, "Why aren't you married?" her reply is simple: "I've never been that interested in marriage." There are decidedly many meaningful things into which a woman can pour herself besides a husband and children. A woman's freedom to make this decision is one of the great and unprecedented privileges of living in the West today. But it seems like most single women I've known, somewhere between the ages of twenty-eight and thirty-two, if not before, start asking the *why* question and grope—some more doggedly than others—for answers. So we are brought full circle to the girlfriends' coffee klatch.

At the end of the day, you and your friends might approach the question from a hundred different angles. You can evaluate men and the reasons for their passivity, their seeming crises of personal authority, and their assorted fears. You can analyze the divorce culture and how it has damaged and scared many younger people. You can investigate how the freedom (and sometimes compulsion) for women to have careers has changed how the genders perceive and relate to one another. You can get a therapist and explore your own history, issues, desires, and expectations around men, marriage, sexuality, intimacy, etc. You can stand on a mountaintop and beg with a guttural yell for God's explanation. You can take a long, hard look at your dress size, body language, calendar, and social skills. And if you are not too utterly exhausted after all of this, you can make some changes. Get out more, update your hairstyle, practice being a little more vulnerable, steward your sexual wares more wisely, pray more, and quite possibly, genuinely enjoy the growth and change.

Still, all the analysis and restructuring in the world might not get you what you want, including a satisfying answer to the *why* question. I mean, you might come to understand what has wrought the four Bostons full of single women. You may grow to understand why it would have been a total disaster for you to end up with Dave or Eddie or whomever. You might even discover that your singleness has nothing to do with your relative greatness or lack thereof. But you still might not know why *you* are single or why your best friend or younger sister isn't living in the "four Bostons" with you. You might understand that the world is fallen and often unfair, but that's still not the kind of answer that warms you on a lonely Saturday night. And if in your heart of hearts you still yearn to be married or have a family, this hard mystery lives, eats, and sleeps with you.

A few years ago, I was in Vancouver, Canada, for a work-related conference. I took the occasion to spend one free evening with an older Scottish couple, Jim and Rita Houston, with whom I had lived while in graduate school. Though we hadn't kept up since then, I always had a warm spot in my heart for them, built on fond memories of Sunday afternoon family lunches (five students lived with the Houstons at the time), games of Scrabble in front of the fire, and incisive comments from each of them. Mrs. Houston was a practical, matter-of-fact woman: "Dearie, it's better to be single and wish you were married than to be married and wish you were single!" She had a good point. Dr. Houston, who looked like a clean-cut, twinkly-eyed Santa Claus, was a professor of spiritual theology at the college. His words: "As you grow, you will discover that your personhood is more important than your personality." I always nodded with a twenty-three-year-old's faith that one day I'd actually know what he was talking about.

Thirteen years later, I was once again in their home, eating Scottish food and playing Scrabble. During the evening, we chatted about my work, mutual friends, our families, and the direction that the college was going. To my surprise and perhaps relief, nobody mentioned my marital status, and the conversation remained pleasant and easy. Then, at a reasonable hour (the Houstons were now both in their mid to upper seventies), Dr. Houston suggested he drive me back to my hotel. Mrs. Houston and I bid each other good-bye.

I can't remember what we were discussing at the moment, but as we moved through the numbered streets, Dr. Houston quietly spoke. "You've suffered much being single." I couldn't tell if he was asking me or telling me. "Um, well, um, well . . . I . . ." I stammered like a person who'd just gotten a wave of indigestion. In fact, that word *suffered* had hit something in my guts. "I am sorry," he said in the silence.

It was strange, his use of the word *suffer*. It seemed a bit dramatic. I mean, isn't suffering when you have a horrible disease, lose a family member in a car wreck, or starve in a famine? Isn't that what it is to really suffer? I decided to shake it off. More silence. Then he continued. "Your mother, too; she has suffered in your singleness." Now he was getting in my business. I watched the storefronts and their neon signs whiz by in a blur as we drove through downtown Vancouver; I was ready to be at the hotel. I tightened my stomach, trying to muffle the chord his words had struck.

"Well, yeah, I think it was really hard on her at first, because it messed up her vision of her daughter's ideal life. And then I think her sadness switched to just being disappointed on my behalf, you know, like any mom would be sad to see her daughter's desires go unmet." And then I quickly added—as if to say, *But let's not get all grim about this; you know there is a silver lining in the cloud*—"But I think it has made me appreciate my parents more and grow closer to them than I otherwise would have."

"Yes, yes," he quietly concurred. "Of course that's good." He was looking at the road through the windshield, and I now joined him, staring straight ahead. *Come on, hotel.* "The question, of course," he continued, "is *how* will you suffer? Will you suffer with bitterness or will you suffer prophetically?" *O Lord, I don't like how this sounds.* "You see, your generation is experiencing the fallout of a culture profoundly confused about who God is and therefore about what it is to be human and what it is to love. Your relational disappointments and suffering are, sadly, emblematic of the age."

It suddenly seemed like he was speaking from a vantage point I didn't want to share. I didn't want to be the poster child for some cosmic cultural crisis. I wanted a manageable, fixable problem. "Well, I have tried to work on any issues I might have."

"Yes, yes," he gently agreed without dropping the matter, "though I imagine that has only made things worse. You've kept growing, and most of the men around you have not. So the gap and perhaps the sense of suffering from isolation get greater." *Please God, get me to the hotel quickly.*

Suddenly, it appeared—a seeming sanctuary—and we pulled into the driveway. *Finally.* He turned now to look at me. I tried to smile an *oh yes—emblematic of the age—what a shame—oh well, whatever—I'm sure the right guy will come along for me shortly—thanks for dinner* kind of smile. He looked at me pleasantly, as if patiently waiting for my internal monologue to cease. Then, with more compassion than I wanted for a level of suffering and vision that I decidedly did not want, he looked at me with the kind of warmth that burns away every fiber of defense standing between me and the pain of an unanswered *why*. "Connally, like the prophets of old, take the pain—which is also the pain of this culture—to the Lord. Seek his heart of love and direction for yourself and for others." He paused, and in spite of my tightest belly and my most clenched jaw, his words got in and tears quietly spilled out. "Perhaps I can pray for you now?" he suggested.

He prayed. I gave him a quick hug, thanked him for dinner, and tried to hop merrily out of the car. (Sometimes I'm ridiculous about not wanting to cry in public.) I smiled dimly at a few colleagues lingering in the hotel lobby and headed straight for my room. By the time I got to my floor, the tears were gushing. I think I spent the rest of that night in quasi-escape mode. I watched *Braveheart* on my laptop DVD player, the high drama of the movie giving me an outlet for the inarticulate pathos churned up in me.

In retrospect, it was strange what that conversation with Dr. Houston did to and for me. Somehow, in linking the word "suffer" to my unintentionally single state, he legitimized something at work in my guts, some pain that I wanted to avoid for very good reasons, like: nothing is more depressing than some old, whiny, lonely spinster; it could be worse (I could be married and wish I weren't); it's not as if there have been no men whatsoever—it has been my choice to say no to a few along the way; and lastly, what would be the point of going *there?* To sit around and bellyache? But in calling it "suffering," he was legitimizing a part of me that did ache at sleeping alone every night. And the simple acknowledgment—having the ache compassionately seen and known by another—did its own quiet, little miracle. Something in my guts unclenched.

More than that, however, Dr. Houston's words flipped my *why* question on its head and left me asking, *What now? How then should I live?* I wasn't sure what living prophetically meant (images of wild-haired, wide-eyed, angry men came to mind), but I knew at minimum it meant living in the truth. It meant admitting that the confusion plaguing me (and so many of the men and women around me) was real and not easily navigated. It meant owning my unmet desires and the related disappointment. And it also meant holding on to and holding up the goodness and the realness of God in the midst of it. Dr. Houston's words about suffering prophetically had felt like a gut-level punch. But in reality, they were more like the compassion-induced Heimlich maneuver, freeing me to live.

It is worth considering this question of *How then should I live?* I'm not talking about asking yourself, *How then should I get a man?* Or *How then should I explain my singleness?* Or even *How then should I prepare for life alone?* Those questions have some merit, but they are secondary. Rather, I'm talking about asking for your eyes to be opened to see what's real and then learning how to move forward in reality, even if it's wading one step at a time through periodic waves of tears. Your steps will likely be different from mine or from any of the other four-Boston residents. They could lead anywhere—to quiet, hidden, heart places or to large, dramatic, public stages. To marriage, to a single life. To home owner-ship, to a rented apartment. To a meaning-filled career or "just a job" that pays the bills. Most recently, my steps have led me to risk en-trusting my Saturday nights to God. It might sound like a really small example, but it's one of the toughest things in the world for me. Just combine an extrovert hungry for intimacy with a lot of songs running around in her head about Saturday nights—there are a lot out there—and the outcome is obvious. She can be one lonely and dissatisfied chick on the weekends. So instead of numbing out, I'm asking God to step into my Saturday night scene. I have no idea where that request will lead. But I'm up for the adventure.

Last spring I was in Colorado for another conference. I spent one lunch hour with Esther, a wise and beautiful African woman, who in her fifties, is still single. She is the sort of woman whose eyes make me want to trade secrets. Our conversation meandered from work to men. "Esther," I asked, "do you think you've been called to be single?" She sat, quiet, and looked at me with one of those Dr. Houston kind of looks (maybe there was something similar in the water of Scotland and Kenya that each of these two drank growing up). With a lilt in her voice she said, "Yes, Connally, for today I am called to be single. I cannot say about tomorrow."

For today I am called to be single. I cannot say about tomorrow. That is how I want to live: not anxiously asking why but simply looking for what is supposed to be for today. I think of the story about Jesus with the man who was born blind. Jesus' disciples were concerned with figuring out why this man was blind—whose issue was to blame, so to speak. "Who," they wanted to know, "sinned . . . causing him to be born blind?" Jesus' response always amazes me: "You're asking the wrong question. You're looking for someone to blame. There is no such cause-effect here. Look instead for what God can do."[38] Or as another version puts it, "Neither this man nor his parents sinned. . . . This happened so that the work of God might be displayed in his life."[39] And then Jesus demonstrated that in fact God is at work today; he miraculously healed the guy.

Sometimes I think that one of the primary works God has done in my life is to tenderize and enrich my heart through the "Why aren't I married?" struggle—the suffering I still hesitate to call by that name for fear of others rolling their eyes. But instead of the disappointment leaving me a cold, bitter, angry wench or a hotly desperate man-eater, it's wrought a heart more capable of and committed to giving and receiving love. That, in my estimation, is miracle-level material. And though anything might happen tomorrow, that is the work of God I've seen today.

Given all this, wouldn't it be something if the next time someone asked you, "So, why aren't you married?" you paused, looked him or her in the eye, and then quietly replied, "Honestly, the bottom line is pretty simple. The reason I'm not married is so that today the work of God might be displayed in my life."

That would be quite the answer. It wouldn't be a snappy one, but it just might be the truth.

CHAPTER 14

Dancing Shoes

Inevitably, sometime between November and Christmas each year a major TV network airs the now-classic movie *The Sound of Music*. And if it's the uncut version, the opening scene will be delightfully long—a panoramic sweep of Salzburg, Austria, and the surrounding countryside, complete with dazzling orchestral accompaniment. Then, as the overture moves toward its crescendo, the camera narrows in on a green field atop an Austrian foothill. There, with arms outstretched and drenched in sunshine, Julie Andrews as Maria is revealed, dancing and spinning with abandon, the snowcapped Alps her only visible audience. With perfect timing, the camera zooms in on Maria as she spins toward the lens and begins to sing her famous song: "The hills are alive with the sound of music. . . ."

As goofy as the whole movie seems to some people (one boyfriend of mine spent hours mocking my love of that movie), the truth is, I see those Austrian Alps, hear that music swell, watch Maria spin, and joy gushes up in me every time.

Since I was a little girl, that type of joy image—abandoned singing and swirling to a backdrop of majestic beauty—has always compelled me. It hasn't always characterized me, but it has always beckoned me. I've "known in my knower" that joy is there, even when it has eluded my radar screen of feelings. But when I hit my early thirties and smacked headlong into my unmet desires for both a husband and meaningful vocation (preferably in that order), my faith faltered and a sneaking suspicion crept in: Perhaps that joy would never be mine. Underneath this suspicion was the unspoken belief that marriage, sex, and kids (preferably in that order) were the path to ultimate adulthood joy—something I was intrinsically cut out of as a single woman.

A few years later, when I could talk about all this with a bit more freedom, I discovered that others had wrestled with similar thoughts. My friend Lindsay recounts her story:

> Sometime in my mid to late twenties, just as my singleness was starting to make me nervous, my mom asked me if I wanted to have a piece of art that had hung in my room while I was growing up. It was four little paintings framed in one long gold frame. . . . The first of the little paintings was of a young woman with a man kneeling in front of her; underneath there was a caption that read "The Betrothal." The second was of the same young woman in front of a trunk overflowing with lace and turn-of-the-century gowns. Its caption read "The Trousseau." The third was "Their New Home" and showed the young woman serving her husband dinner. The fourth was "Their New Love" and showed the two newlyweds hovering over a bassinet. The title over all four paintings was "The Greatest Moments of a Girl's Life." When my mom offered to

let me take it back to my house in DC, I told her, "No thanks. According to this thing I haven't had any of the greatest moments of a girl's life, and that's depressing."

In retrospect, it's not that anyone overtly declared to me there was no joy to be had as a single, celibate woman. It's just that like many of us, I secretly believed that the *deepest drafts* are to be drunk only by those invited to a joy party. And the only people invited to that party are those walking in the marriage/sex/kids shoes. Too bad for me or anyone else stuck wearing these unsought single shoes. The bouncer would take one look at my feet and never let me into the party, even if my favorite movie is *The Sound of Music*.

The problem (and ironically, also the good news) was that I was wrong. Subtly but undeniably wrong. The gift of consummate joy is not out of reach for the single woman any more than it is guaranteed for the married woman. The snafu is that many of us (including married women) lodge our hope for consummate joy in the hope of betrothal, trousseau, new home, and new bundle. I, for one, secretly bowed before these ideals, and in return, these heavy stone idols sat on my chest, squeezing the air out of my lungs.

Of course, the solution isn't to fill the frame instead with pictures of a girl holding her first diploma, her first pay stub, her first mortgage payment, or her first award for civic contribution. I have some friends who don't see marriage as for them and instead have decided to bank their joy on their professional accomplishments. But while any particular set of the pictures might be a *means* of great joy, no one picture or even collage of pictures is life's ultimate *source* of joy. Mistaking the two can land any of us in very deep weeds, far from the Austrian mountaintops.

I say this now with a greater clarity and conviction than I did a few years ago. It has taken me a while to get this "source of joy" thing straight. The struggle is probably half of what this book is about. And even now, I must be reminded of what's true in a myriad of ways from a myriad of sources.

But what about this ultimate source of joy? What exactly is it? And where exactly is it found?

Others have written extensively on this subject with far greater insight and fluidity than I'll ever possess. I'm tempted, therefore, simply to subcontract out the rest of the chapter—you know, find someone who can speak to a complex and cynical age in a way that makes sophisticated sense. But at the risk of sounding like a clichéd bumper sticker, I'm just going to say it: *There's one true, if mysterious, source of inexpressible and glorious joy: the triune God—Father, Son, and Holy Spirit—aka the Joy Maker.*

Actually, I don't think that is a cliché, but part of me would like there to be another answer, because this one makes some people nervous. It is so universal, absolute, and a little out-there for your average, educated North American. Part of me would love to say, "Oh, no problem, joy is found wherever you want it to be—on Match.com or in a glass of fine merlot or spinning on a mountaintop." And of course, joy is often found in those places. But even these joys proceed from a Joy with a capital J. Bach summed it up well when he entitled his chorale "Jesu, Joy of Man's Desiring." That desire for joy, that longing I mistakenly believed could only *really* be met with a marriage/sex/kids ticket has as its ultimate object and therefore its source something deeper and more eternal: Jesus. And the amazing thing about this is that if we want him, regardless of our marital status or anything else, we'll never be cut out of his joy party.

For more reasons than I can name here, this truth about Jesus as the *source of joy* is embarrassingly hard for me to believe. But as I've risked putting my real weight on it (not secretly keeping one toe on other ground), I've found that this truth is strong enough to hold the whole me, met and unmet desires alike. A soft, flimsy truth would have collapsed by now.

And I am not alone in this. Another friend talks about her discovery of the source of joy:

> [When I thought about the source of Joy,] my first thoughts were about my accomplishments—living overseas, getting out of a bad relationship even though it was hard to do, making a CD, struggling with performance anxiety long enough to see progress. . . . But if I shuck it down as to why those things brought me joy, it's because I see God as the source of it. So, to sound very Sally Spiritual—my greatest source of joy is to see God do something in, around, or through my life. I'm reassured of his presence, his grace, and his affections for me. That brings me a deeper joy that can't be gained anywhere else—oh, and I did have these two kittens that brought me joy!

Can we go back for a moment to *The Sound of Music*? If you've ever seen it, you might remember Mother Superior. She's the woman with a big, soft, velvety pink face peering out of her black and white habit. She's the one who speaks firmly but kindly to nun-in-training Maria when Maria's blossoming romance with the handsome Captain von Trapp seems to be ended. "Maria," says Mother Superior, framed by a stained-glass backdrop, "when God shuts a door, he opens a window."

I think if Mother Superior and I had met during my early thirties, she would have had some words for me. I can picture it: me moaning in a heap in front of a door blocked by a bouncer, who is declaring, "Sorry, lady. Wrong shoes. No joy party for you." Mother Superior walks up to me in her habit. "Honey, stop banging on the marriage door thinking you're shut out of joy. Head out the window that is open for you now. God can deliver real joy anywhere." Of course, I probably wouldn't have heard her, thinking she just didn't get it. After all, she *wanted* to be a nun.

It's a moot point, however, because Mother Superior wasn't there in my early thirties. There were, though, other real voices of encouragement—male and female, older and younger. I think in large part due to these friends' promptings and reminders of the truth, I found the courage to admit, *Hey, this door is not currently open,* and to crawl out over that windowsill. In short, I was finally able to meet the Joy Maker on *his* terms.

If life were a Broadway musical, at this moment I'd begin belting out a song about what I've found over the rainbow or about impossible dreams coming true. But it's not, so I won't. Still, I will say this: Crawling over that windowsill, I've discovered that the ground on the other side is solid, if not always smooth or soft. Maybe *everything* isn't suddenly coming up roses and daffodils, but I am once again humming Broadway tunes—to the chagrin of a few people. And an unknown future, instead of giving me a wave of anxiety, almost makes me giddy with anticipation (okay, *almost*).

Before I continue, however, I must ask a question. Do you think it's possible to find real, dance-inducing joy as a woman with an unmet desire for marriage? Or sex? Or kids? Or a dream job? Or something else? Honestly, what do you believe down in your most secret center? It's worth stopping for a minute or an hour—or a year—to wrestle with this question, because your answer affects everything.

My own struggle with this question must be obscenely evident. Writing this chapter has been hard for me because my yearning for joy is so relentlessly woven—rightly and wrongly, I think—into my wrestling with singleness. Even yesterday I got tired of thinking about it, quit writing, snarfed down dark chocolate, and went for a walk.

Treading down a quiet mountain road, my sunglasses on my head and my ponytail flopping behind me, I noticed how the late afternoon sun was shining at an angle through the trees. It cast long shadows broken by erratic patches of warm light. As I walked through those light patches, I felt the sun on my tie-dyed T-shirt and caught its radiant brightness with the corner of my eye. But, one moment later, I was in the shadows again, the sun blocked. C. S. Lewis called this world we live in "the shadowlands." I'm not sure if this is exactly what he meant, but as I walked down that country road, the light-and-shadow pattern suddenly reminded me of the interplay of joy with life. Much of life is walked in shadows, the sometimes painful uncertainty that necessitates faith. Even so, there are moments when we walk through the warm light, recognizing real joy and glimpsing the *source* of joy out of the corner of our eyes.

There's a book on singleness titled *Sassy, Single, and Satisfied*.[40] I love that title because it connotes a vision of the single woman I would like to be. I want to sport a Prada bag while possessing perfect legs, full lips, and hair that is appropriately swingy. I want to carry myself with tanned confidence in a black bikini (my epitome of sassy). And I want to live with my heart so full of love and my talents so well used that hundreds of people are served (my definition of satisfied). But between here and there—as my knockoff designer bag and I walk through the shadowlands of diets, dates, dullness, and drama—I ask the Joy Maker to help me recognize more of who he is and what he offers.

The funny thing is, he is answering that prayer. Before writing this chapter, I took a "joy inventory" to see if I could honestly say I was experiencing any deep or even shallow joy in my life. If I couldn't, then I really would have to find a ghostwriter. While the inventory didn't use up my computer's entire memory, I did generate a couple of solid pages. And though I know that joy comes differently for each person, I want to share a few examples simply because they are real.

Laughing about singleness. This one amazes me. Of course I still desire to be married, but with the secret suspicions about being cut out of real joy put in their place, unsought singleness is not without its humor or fun. I'm thinking of a game my dear childhood friend Polly and I made up recently while we were both home for the holidays. Waiting for our dinner at a restaurant, we invented and played a game: Match the Ex-Boyfriends. Though I can't remember how one technically "won," it was simple to play. We began by listing on our respective napkins all the guys we'd gone out with since seventh grade. Then we compared, looking for matches.

"Okay, let's see. Kind of math-y, introverted, into computers. Um . . . I think I'll have to go with Clint. How about you?" Polly studied her list. "Definitely, it's Jake. But how about hot, soul-touching, and utterly incapable of commitment?" I looked my list over. "Girl, you know the answer: Nate." She rolled her eyes. "Of course, I just wish I'd met him! Well, Rusty would be mine. So, do you have any narcissists on your list?" "Narcissists? Oh! I think have two, and I'll raise you one guy with white socks and dark shoes."

How the game ended I don't know, but we ended up howling over stories of horrendous blind dates, our own silly choices, and the inscrutability of life. By the time dessert came, I realized I'd walked through a warm light patch, and glimpsing the source, I remembered to thank him.

On the inventory I also noted "panty hose races down the hallway." That's when you and your friend roll your panty hose down to your ankles and run for the finish line. Also making the cut was "Ben and Jerry's ice cream—with candle—for Dolly's birthday breakfast." Nothing like fudge chunks in bed at 7:00 a.m. to make a girl happy! And there was "smashing the tennis ball as hard as I could in a game with Holly, who never ran, never sweated, always chuckled, and always won." (Yes, I really do have friends named Polly, Dolly, and Holly. And there's also Molly and Lolly. Come on, you know that's a little warm patch too.)

But as grateful as I am for the crazy laughter, something deeper and even closer to capital J joy has also showed up on this side of the windowsill. As I alluded to before, part of lugging myself over that windowsill was acknowledging that it (life, men, marriage, sex, kids, work, whatever) isn't all about me and my terms. I still forget this on a regular basis—as in daily. But the shocking delight has been to discover—and rediscover—the real joys of joining with God in *his* creative purposes. It comes from being a part of, as my friend Steph calls it, "something undeniably grand."

For some, those purposes include building a marriage and a family (which takes some serious, if rewarding, labor). I'm not going to lie; I still hope I'll get to do that in some form or fashion. I've watched my brothers with their families. My older brother and his wife have led the way with great parenting of sweet, fun-loving sons. Eating burgers, watching movies, and riding waves on boogie boards with them can bring joy down to my toes. I can exhale when I'm with my brothers' families. But as good as all of that feels—and it's not perfect, but good—today I am saying to the Joy Maker, "Show me who *you* are and show me how *you* want to use me." So far I've seen that connecting and working with him—like trekking down that country road—is a journey laced with joy. And the joy is real.

I remember the phone call I received from Talisha, a young African-American student of mine, who wanted to thank me for a recent class discussion. It was the first time she'd felt safe enough to "really go there" in a discussion with her predominantly white peers about racial tension in the high school. That thrilled my heart. Or I think of the chance I had to see Cara explore and discover who Jesus is as she read portions of the New Testament with a group of other women explorers. I fumbled along as a facilitator whose faith got to grow in the process. And I remember the incredible experience it was to exercise my latent Broadway impulses as a co-emcee for a conference of 1,200 people. Toby, my co-emcee, and I honestly sought to serve the conferees. But admittedly, the standing ovation at the end elicited our ear-to-ear grins. There can be joy in a job well done.

Joining the Joy Maker in his work can take on so many different forms. It can be changing a baby's diaper, hitting the right notes in a song, taking a friend to get his wisdom teeth removed, running an office well, getting to know that seventy-five-year-old neighbor, or working on a task force for the Department of Justice. There are endless opportunities around us if we'll risk discovering them.

Sometimes participation entails being on the receiving end of the Joy Maker's work. I cried tears of joy when one friend spontaneously raised money to cover my unexpected April tax burden. I smiled from my heart when I came home to balloons sent by another friend to celebrate my book contract signing. And the hours of labor people have given to help me move my things in and out of homes and storage? It awes me.

Still, if the chapter ended here, it might be misleading. It might sound as if the tastes of real joy in life come solely from our doing or being done to. *So, you can't build a marriage and kids? No worries. Work harder and build a department, a ministry, a portfolio, or a network of loving friends.* It would be a good start, but it would still be missing something crucial. In the end, we'd just be filling up the gold frame with a revised four-picture set.

Earlier I said that the desire for joy has as its ultimate object and source something deeper and more eternal—Jesus. I've made it the whole way through the chapter, without a subcontractor I might add, and I still believe it's true. I know, though, that I haven't made a complete case for *how* it is true. Let's face it, I'm not a lawyer. But I can lay my hand on the Bible and, as one random witness, simply swear to tell the whole truth and nothing but the truth, so help me God.

So what might Jesus as the source of joy look like?

When all the doing and being done to has subsided, and when desire has wafted, met and unmet, over and through me, this is what remains: The mountains and the stars still declare God's voice, *I am here.* The Communion bread and wine cutting down into my guts declare, *Your bottomless pit of muck and sin has been redeemed.* The words "I have loved you with an everlasting love; I have drawn you with loving-kindness. . . .

Again you will . . . go out to dance with the joyful"[41] continue to re-sound inside me. Though written some 2,500 years ago for other people, I can't help but know that they are also for me, now. And in response to all this—the stars, the wine, the words—grateful joy grows in my soul, and I thank a triune God for being real and awe-inspiring. This is nothing but the truth.

So, what's my point? I think it's the same as Mother Superior's. God really is there, and though he shuts doors, he also opens windows. And regardless of which portal he opens, on the other side is ground solid enough to dance on—to dance on with him, the triune Joy Maker. Gratefully, the shoes we wear don't matter—we are invited to start moving our imperfect feet.

Such a concept is a million miles from what I was believing when I hit my early thirties and felt joy threatening to slip away. It's actually far from what I felt two Saturday nights ago. But I'm thankful that the problem is just my capacity to forget truth when the shadows are too long. The truth is, unmet desire has not turned out to be the death of joy; instead it has led to a more dogged search and discovery. And what I've found is that if we risk joining the dance despite the shadows, every now and then we will spin into some decidedly warm patches of light. Then out of the corner of our eyes we'll catch a glimmer of the *source*. And without a shadow of a doubt, we will "know in our knower" that in spite of unmet desires, late fees from the bank, steep housing costs, tough bosses, and goofy guys, the Joy Maker is and will be eternally real.

CHAPTER 15

When Good Friends Marry Off

When good friends—male or female—get married, so much changes. I first discovered this when one of my best friends since seventh grade, Mary Ellen (aka Melon), tied the knot. She married a guy whom she, another best friend, and I had palled around with in high school. As a result, everything shifted. Suddenly Scott was Melon's husband more than he was our friend, and Melon was less available because, as we once joked, she had a lot of work to do fixing up Scott! But when you're twenty-four and this happens, it is okay. This is normal; it's what is supposed to happen. Besides, there are a zillion fun young people out there with whom you might be friends, and you probably figure your turn is coming soon.

When your turn doesn't come, however, and when you are a bridesmaid in yet another wedding (I'm up to double digits as of this

writing, including two in the next three months), letting go of another close friendship—or at least watching it dramatically change—
can get a little, well, old. And the temptation can be to put weddings,
or the people who might want you to be in theirs one day, on the
shelf. If you fight the temptation and continue to engage with new
friends, chances are you'll end up in the same boat again. People will
move, girlfriends will get husbands and children, and you might still
be single and feeling the loss. So what does it look like to value intimacy in friendships while still letting friends leave? And how do you
do that when you really wish you were moving to married-land yourself? Sometimes, I think, you just figure it out as you go.

As I sat on the stairs of the public library with my friend Del, we
slowly reviewed the history of our friendship. We'd been roommates
for a short while when I first moved to town, and having instantly
clicked, we hung out and touched base regularly for two years. We
even had "Sunday school hour" together, a regularly scheduled nine
o'clock breakfast in a Philly café before our respective church ser-
vices. I'd since moved to DC, but we had stayed in constant touch,
catching up with good long chats, even exchanging handwritten
notes and cards. The distance changed the expression but not the
content of our mutual affection. Then Glenn entered the equation.

I had prayed with Del long and hard for this man. Her longing for
him had been brewing for a year, and finally, one January afternoon
when I was back in Philly visiting, we got down on our knees, literally,
and prayed our guts out. We asked that either Glenn would move toward her definitively or that she'd get unhooked from her desire. To
my complete amazement (sometimes my faith is skimpy), she got a
call the very next day: He was ready to go for it.

A big grin remained plastered on each of our faces for a long time.
But inevitably, that entrance of Glenn—whom I delightfully took to
as my new friend-in-law—shifted things in a way that geographic distance hadn't. Del's heart was reorienting, focusing in a new and exclu-

sive way, and we both knew it. Shortly after they were engaged, I visited again. That's when we sat on those public library steps. We spoke about what we had valued in our friendship over the years, what we appreciated about one another, and how all her relationships were shifting. Glenn was to be her number one relational priority, and she wanted to do whatever she could to help their upcoming marriage fly with love and health. I concurred; I would want the same if I were in her shoes. In short, this meant that she'd be asking less of our friendship and that she'd be giving less. We briefly prayed together, gave each other a hug, and called it a chapter. Everything was right and peaceful, but at that moment, it felt like another loss. And at thirty-three that loss felt a little deeper than it did at twenty-four. One more deep connection cultivated and then cut back.

Not long after, I went through a similar experience with my younger brother. Though Robert had lived overseas since college, he had always been my closest guy friend, particularly as I moved past that magical year of thirty. Perhaps we were close because he was four years younger and we had therefore bypassed a lot of competition and conflict growing up. Maybe it was a shared childhood history of wearing small plaid blazers and homemade badges while playing "FBI," or his standing on the ottoman while I danced around him in endless circles. Or maybe it was because he is empathetic, real, and always cracking me up, especially as our older brother had been married several years and we were the remaining single adults together. Regardless, it was a tight enough friendship for me to travel to Syria to see him; to travel with him through India, Thailand, and Hong Kong; and for me to visit him in Beirut.

On one of my trips to see Robert when he was in grad school at the American University of Beirut, we joined a group of his friends for a weekend getaway. Piled into the overloaded van of one of his newfound friends, Danny, we ventured into the mountains to see the few remaining cedars of Lebanon, ancient trees now doggedly protected by the Lebanese government. I knew nobody on the trip except my brother, but for the most part, people were friendly. Conversation spun around in both English and Arabic, and when I wanted something translated, I'd just tap my brother on his knee and say, "What does that mean?"

The trees were worth seeing, and all went well enough on the weekend until the return trip. Not only was Danny—a long-haired, Lebanese James Dean type—a bit loose at the wheel (driving on the "closed for construction" section of the highway while talking animatedly with his hands) but Robert and another of his new friends, Chantal, got lost together in the last seat of the van. Cooing and giving foot rubs, they spent the entire trip home utterly absorbed in one another. This might have been okay had I a history with some of the other people, had the van not been careening around curves at eighty miles per hour, or had more of the conversation been in English. But there I sat. My best guy friend (and translator) was lovestruck in the backseat while I stared out the window, white-knuckled.

The thing is, even after knowing her for only twenty-four hours, I liked Chantal. Her whimsical Aussie accent (ethnically Lebanese, she'd been raised primarily in Sydney), her big smile, and her relentless passion were heartwarming. Even her denim-skirted, combat-booted, slightly grunge look was endearing on her petite frame. (Being five feet ten, I would look scary in combat boots—like a militant Amazon woman.) I just didn't like the bursts of jealousy flaring up in me. So after my pitiful and failed attempts to get my brother's attention with distinctly American sarcasm, I reminded myself I was USA-bound in twenty-four hours, and all would be well.

That evening, my brother and I had a brief van trip deconstruction chat. "See, Con," he explained, "I was just speaking her love language of touch by rubbing her feet! Letting her know I care about her on her terms." "All about service, eh?" was my eye-rolling response. But my cheekiness fell on deaf ears. I could tell he was hooked. So the next day when Chantal and I said our good-byes, I affirmed to her my brother's trustworthiness. In spite of my van ride jealousy, I knew I'd also seen a flame actually worth fanning. Then off I went to the airport. A few hours and seven security checkpoints later, gazing down on Beirut out of the airplane window, I knew this was it for my brother. Something was going to have to shift in our relationship too.

The shift didn't fully register until a number of months later when I made a trip to another continent, Australia—this time for Robert and Chantal's wedding. Perhaps it was jet lag and fatigue, but after the rehearsal dinner, I sat on the moderately clean hotel room floor and broke down. I cried because I knew the special exclusivity in my brother's and my friendship was changing; my number one champion now had someone else to champion above me. I cried because there was an intimacy transfer going on, and I felt like I was the loser. I cried because it was my little brother getting married; I was now the left-behind spinster sister. And I cried, thoroughly humiliated that I was such a ridiculous drama queen.

Under duress, however, even drama queens can bend their knees. So I found myself literally kneeling, asking for help. "Help me, please, God, to let my brother go. Fill the gap in my heart. Enable me to let Chantal take her rightful place. Amen."

Letting go is never easy under any circumstances, but I think it feels more difficult when it seems like you're letting someone go toward *more* and you are being left behind with *less*. (Though friends in difficult marriages remind me that sometimes less is more.) In any case, what other choice is there besides letting go? Getting angry? Getting clingy? Getting detached? Throwing a self-pity party to be beat all pity parties? There are elements of short-term pleasure in each, but none of them will do the real trick: i.e., keep the loss at bay. Nope, letting go with grace is the only way forward.

What does it look like, letting go with grace? I imagine that there are many manifestations, but I think it can look a little like this: being willing to face the ugly, empty, scared parts of your own soul—no matter how ridiculous or embarrassing—and naming them aloud. Usually for me this sounds something like telling God and a friend, "I'm insanely jealous and feel highly ripped off and left out."

Then there's asking for the help to change. Maybe even wrestling with God and your own soul long and hard enough until he blesses you with the capacity to say honestly and joyfully to a dear friend, "Congratulations! I am so happy for you!" And sometimes, along the way, you might just need to march forward with a little pain.

I remember coming home late one evening, noticing the house was pitch black but that my roommate's soon-to-be-fiancé's car was out front. A sinking feeling came over me. One can only walk into a dark house with one's roommate and her boyfriend cuddled up on the couch in front of the fireplace so many times without starting to feel a bit third-wheely at best or nauseated at worst. Taking a deep breath, I reached for the handle of my car door and then froze. I couldn't get out of my car and go into that house. My heart couldn't take watching Ryan's hand gently caress Dana's as the two of them otherwise graciously attempted to converse with me. Somehow, though our conversation was real enough, each of his curlicue finger motions on her forearm was like a screaming reminder of my own intimate love gaps. And that maxed out my pain-o-meter.

But I didn't want to sleep in my car, and my bed was in that house. So, feeling like an idiot, I called a friend, explained the situation, and declared, "Jeannie, you have to pray me through the door." With great understanding she obliged, and a few minutes later I left my car and, with much banging and clanging, let myself in the front door.

Maybe this is not so much a picture of letting go *with* grace—which somehow connotes effortless, decorous ease—as much as it's an image of letting go *by* grace, which isn't always pretty. Only Someone bigger than I am got me inside that door and able to genuinely engage with Dana and Ryan. Only Someone bigger than I am could keep me from being a royal snot, from copping an attitude of vague disdain toward their shared tenderness. Only Someone bigger than I am could enable me to know in my gut, "This is a good gift my friend has been given. Let her enjoy her gift." I've needed that grace in the crevices of my soul where the temptation to cling and control relentlessly resides.

Actually, nothing has taught me dependence on God like letting go of people. I don't think it's simply because I'm a chronically codependent, enmeshed, dysfunctional relational junkie. Perhaps there's some truth in that. But honestly, letting go can just be hard on the heart, and sometimes I need help. I need help trusting that if, like a trapeze artist, I let go of one swinging ladder and free-fall through the air, another ladder will come to my hand when the time is right. David, the second king of Israel, once said, "I was young and now I am old, yet I have never seen the righteous forsaken or their children begging bread."[42] I wish I could ask him if his observations applied to food for the soul as well as for the body.

I know I have had some serious hunger pains since my friends started marrying off fifteen years ago. There have been many lonely, dateless Saturday nights when I've wanted to call a friend but she's out with her husband. There are annual moments at family beach gatherings when my brothers and their wives go out for long walks and I'm left watching another *Veggie Tales* video with their children and my parents. Honestly, at times it has felt like getting whacked in the heart by an emotional hammer. Strangely though, it's as if the pattern of loss has actually softened my heart. Though I would never have chosen it (and would melt down that hammer if I had the choice), letting go again and again has pounded tenderness into my heart, keeping it from growing leathery and tough. As a result, as crazy as it sounds, my heart has actually grown more fertile.

Somehow, I now have Del and Glenn *and* their two children in my heart. It's like my friendship with Del got reapportioned and then multiplied. Or now, when I connect with my brother, it's far richer and deeper because marriage and fatherhood have left him more patient and tender. Even in letting Dana go to her good gift, my faith in the possibility of good gifts has increased, and hope has swelled my heart. It is as if the cutbacks have in fact spawned more growth.

Recently I went to the post office to pick up my latest bridesmaid dress (one I think I really will wear again). Unboxing it at home and shaking out the wrinkles, a strange thing happened. Instead of freaking out or getting that "I'm stinking sick of being a bridesmaid!" feeling, I found myself quietly smiling, anticipating my friend's wedding day. Miraculously, as the bridesmaid-once-again tried on her dress, the drama queen was at rest. Lingering in the pale blue—not white—dress, I found myself silently concurring with King David: In spite of the real loss of intimacy with many close friends whose lives changed with marriage, I had not been forsaken. I had not been left behind. I had not become an emotional beggar. I was not some pitifully depressing, lonely, old, tight-hearted spinster. To the contrary. As I looked into the mirror, I reflected: My heart was fuller than ever. Something deep in my soul was tasting satisfaction. Plus, my smile grew bigger because, well, between you and me, I thought I looked hot in that dress.

CHAPTER 16

Good Fences Make Good Neighbors

"So, is there something between you and Frank?" asked the secretary, Sandi, in a slightly conspiratorial, tabloidish tone.

"Uh, what do you mean?" I asked, wondering what she was implying about my boss and me.

"You know, are you, like, *with him?*"

"With him? *With* him? With *him?* Not at all! Why would you ask that?" I recoiled as visions of comb-overs danced in my head.

"Well, the last single woman he hired was definitely *with him.*"

Thus began my orientation to downtown professional life.

Admittedly, I started off naive. My dad and his friends were almost always gentlemen, and I entered the world of suits with the assumption that men—at least men that age—would and should be the same. Actually, my boss turned out to be quite respectful, though his off-handed comment about my having modeled threw me for a loop.

"Modeled, Frank? Why do you think I modeled?"

"Oh, I noticed it on your résumé." He was completely sincere.

"My résumé? I don't know what you're talking about."

Turns out I did have the word *modeled* underlined and bolded, as in *Modeled and taught public speaking* as a high school English teacher. Guess his eye didn't wander far enough across the page.

In any case, in numerous interactions with a variety of men, I discovered something that I hadn't been prepared for, at least not emotionally. In the workplace, a single woman is, in the eyes of most men, almost always first and foremost a woman (unless she's worked really hard over time to alter this perception). She's a woman, then a colleague. She's a woman, then a brain. She's a woman, then a human. But definitely, she's a woman. Now, there's nothing wrong with being a woman—actually, I love being a woman—but it comes with a truckload of implications that I didn't learn in advance.

It's not just a question of how to relate to some of those older men at work. There's a bigger question about relating to the entire sphere of *men who have no romantic potential*. How does an "available" woman navigate the wide world of unavailable (or undesirable) men, e.g., most bosses and colleagues, guy friends who are now married, husbands of girlfriends, that stay-at-home dad across the street, etc.? When women married earlier and stayed closer to the nest, they were obviously no less female, but on the whole, they didn't have to navigate as complex a web of multitiered male relationships as my single friends and I do.* My grandmother was a sharp, attractive woman, but I can pretty much bet she was clear on how to relate to most men she encountered. She didn't spend hours figuring out boundaries and levels of appropriate intimacy.

*It does seem to be different for single women. My friend Denise, who is divorced, says this: "Having gone from being married to single has been a real eye-opener for me in terms of men in general. Husbands of my girlfriends are afraid to even look my way some days. Some can and are secure; others seem afraid to even be seen alone with me. Forget playdates (for our kids)—they wouldn't think of doing it now without the wife around. It used to be no problem."

When I surveyed a variety of single girlfriends for their insights, their responses varied, but their language was strikingly similar: "Very interesting dynamics." "Very awkward moments." "His attention became uncomfortable for me." "I've become acutely aware of perceptions." "Proceed with caution." "I became keenly aware of a *vibe*." "Relating to men who are not romantic potentials is tricky." And one, after offering many insights, said, "Wow, I've gone on and on . . . almost like therapy."

Celia, a designer in her mid-twenties, has a feel for the strange new dynamics she has encountered in relating to all kinds of men with no romantic potential. Her response conveys the sense of how complicated it can be.

> What have I learned as a single woman about relating to men? Well, no single guy is "safe," regardless of his age, his religious affiliation—anything that might make you think there's a deterrent. Married men are safe if they want to be . . . and some married men will simply give you the creepy eye, obviously not being the safe version. Older men aren't always grandfatherly; they can be gross, extra creepy. I really don't know how that leaves me relating to them. I know I get to test out my femininity on my male coworkers, know that they respond to me as a woman first—not as a Christian, not as a younger person, but as a woman. And that feels good and right. Most of the time. Is it easy? No. Lines are confusing. . . . Men will hit on you. They will stare at various parts of you that aren't your eyes. Is it always offensive? Not always. I know I'm feminine, and I know when I'm attractive. Do I ever abuse that? Probably. Is it sometimes easier being an attractive, younger woman around men? Yes, and for the wrong reasons. . . . And are family male relationships easier than coworker or male friend

relationships? Not at all. They should be deeper and don't
always feel that way.

Of course, Celia's experiences are situation specific, and she ad-
dresses more relationship categories in one paragraph than I could respond to in one chapter. But her words remind me of what I've come
to see repeatedly: This is yet another mind- and heart-boggling territory, and many of us are map-less.

I'm grateful, though, that some bright single women out there
have traversed the landscape—both professionally and personally—and they do have insights. As I've listened, I've detected a refrain that I've come to see can serve as a compass of sorts. When it
comes to relating to men with no romantic potential, *respect the boundaries and enjoy the benefits.*

For simplicity's sake, let's start with what seems like the obvious
(but often isn't so obvious at a heart level): married men. The most essential starting place is acknowledging one basic reality. While not
every man who lacks romantic potential fits in the "already married"
category, the converse is true. Every man who fits in the already married category "lacks romantic potential." Whether he, she, you, or I
like it or not, he and his wife belong first to each other.

I will die respecting one friend of mine who, when the quite mutual
desire and sexual tension with her married colleague got too strong,
finally asked to be transferred to another city. The pull between Greg
and Sarah was profoundly powerful. But Sarah's conviction about
Greg's intrinsic unavailability was stronger still. She did the gutsy
thing and thereby protected herself, Greg, and his wife. Of course, he
could have had the courage to care for his wife, his marriage, and my
friend—and gotten *himself* transferred—but he didn't, and Sarah didn't
have the luxury of dwelling on that point.

Across the board, all the single women I have known from their
twenties to their forties who have worked with or related meaning-

fully to married men have emphasized the importance of respecting men's marriages and, when possible, meeting their wives. "I meet their wives—so the guys know I *know* they are married and that I respect that relationship." "Knowing their significant others helps me to feel more comfortable relating to them and makes me less threatening in a way." "Relate to couples together, if at all possible." And I might add, "Respect the heart of the wife."

Cindi, a thirty-seven-year-old aspiring musician who also happens to work a government job, tells her story:

> I learned something of this the hard way. I was living in Korea and was involved in a ministry to military personnel. Consequently, I met and was around many men. Most were married, and their wives were back in the States waiting for them to finish their one-year tour. . . . At least one night a week we all got together to play the guitar and sing. Those times included both men and women. I thought it was great. . . . Unfortunately, the wife of one of my guitar-playing friends did not think my friendship with her husband was so great. Phil and I clicked musically, spiritually, and personality-wise. Romantic interest never crossed my mind, and to my knowledge it never crossed his. He spoke very highly of his wife and daughters, bragged on the photos they sent, and missed them terribly. Apparently he mentioned my name one too many times in a phone conversation to his wife, and this created a rift between them that almost ended in divorce. Obviously Phil and his wife had some issues regarding trust, and his friendship with me was like putting a whole truckload of logs on the fire.

The truth is, sometimes we don't know we've crossed boundaries until some serious alarm sounds. Maybe it seems a bit ridiculous—

like the smoke detector is hypersensitive. But that is first and fore-most the married couple's business before it is anyone else's. Re-flecting on her experience, Cindi says she came to see that with married men, common interests, not just a desire for connection, should be the common bond.

> Common interests are both the skeleton and the fuel of the relationship. Without the common interest, the relationship does not exist. It's a blob on the floor. This is in contrast to relationships that have the relationship as the common bond. The relationship itself is the common bond with the fuel being "knowing the other person and being known"— intimacy. It is quite possible to have relationships that are strictly based on something external—a third party, so to say (e.g., work, service, hobbies, etc.). The goal is not to know each other or to build any sort of intimacy; rather, the goal is all about that external thing or third party.

With Phil, Cindi saw in retrospect that though they did have sev-eral common interest bonds, they had also developed a friendship. So when Phil mentioned her in conversation, his wife recognized the *friendship*, not the *common interest* bond, and immediately felt threatened. Eventually, Cindi was able to meet Phil's wife and talk with her. Con-currently, Phil worked (successfully) on saving his marriage. But from that point forward, Cindi and Phil were both conscious of relating around their shared interests—keeping the common interest (not the potential intimacy) the common bond.

At least for some of us, though, all this boundary stuff at our jobs and in friendships is hard work. And sometimes, it's just hard. "Sometimes it breaks my heart," says another woman, Nancy, as she reflected on the changes that her guy friends' marriages have wrought.

I remember receiving a photo of myself in the mail from an old guy friend just after he married. He had taken it when we were in college, and he sent it to me with a note about how it had been on his dresser, making him smile, for years. He thanked me for the years of friendship that he had treasured. Though it felt like he was saying good-bye, we've managed to stay barely in touch. That gesture spoke volumes, though.

That's the funny thing about respecting boundaries. Sometimes it looks more like building a fence, and other times it's more like cutting a tie. Regardless, it's rarely easy—and I can't figure a way around that reality.

There's another aspect to this boundary building that also needs mentioning. When the "meet—or at least respect—the wife" concept is being followed, and when potential sexual tension is at minimum reined in, there is still another side to the boundary discussion. In addition to respecting wives and the power of sexual tension, some of us also need to learn to respect ourselves and what we have to offer. I know that sounds like something from "Dr. Shrink's Recipes for Self-Esteem," but I think it's true. Sometimes the best defense *is* a good offense.

For example, Carol admits that sometimes if the conversation is work-related she finds it "difficult to disagree with [older men]." She tends to see them through the "dad grid," which is great when discussing nonwork things (like their history or life passions) but can make challenging older men in a professional context trickier. On one hand, she's prone to rebel against any authority that even faintly smells of heavy-handedness or injustice. On the other hand, knowing this is her tendency, she sometimes overcompensates and gets too quiet. Simply offering the true content of what she thinks—not just in defiance of the suspect system but as a helpful if not always welcomed contribution—is labor. But not only does it keep her safer and intact, it also helps her workplace grow more honest, just, and effective.

In a different scenario, Nancy has noticed that most of the men in her workplace are safe but "feel weird about me. . . . They think I should find a nice guy and go have babies." Having good boundaries with these men entails owning that while she'd like to marry, she is where she is, and she has something valuable to offer. In essence, the "third party" or "common interest" that she and her male colleagues share (in this case, marketing) is something to which she presently brings valuable abilities, regardless of her marital status. When they can all focus on this, playing offense *together*, some of that latent weirdness inevitably melts away.

Lastly, it is worth mentioning the need for boundaries with those available but undesirable men. Much has been written on this in a variety of books on dating and relationships, but I think it can be summed up simply. As Cindi says, "Clarify, clarify, clarify." With those guy friends in whom you have no real interest, respect them enough to communicate this, even if it's nonverbally. It can be tempting, otherwise, to mentally save a guy or two for a rainy day, keeping the options—real or imagined—open. You know—like you might pick at leftovers not because you like cold spaghetti but just because you're growing hungry. This approach just seems to foster selfishness and gets nobody anywhere.

Oh, and on those really creepy guys with whom there is not only no romantic potential but who actually make your skin crawl? Respect your gut. Some women know how to send the "don't mess with me" vibe. Others bend over backward to make even the creepy guys feel wanted. Such a pattern landed me a quasi-stalker who began phoning repeatedly, invoking the "God has led me to call you" line and basically freaking me out. It took a formalized letter with a reference to the police, copied to my father and the leadership of the church where I met him, to nip that in the bud. So now I'm clear on this: If he creeps you out, get out. And based on my experience with this man, beware of men in ascots in the church pew behind you!

Okay, enough on the boundary thing. All this talk about keeping the lines clear—about where I will or won't go or what I have to offer—can't simply be about staking out territory as an end in itself. That's a sort of life-squelching thought, at least to me. *I've built my fence, I've flown my flag, and here I stand: Pure. Protected. Productive. Isolated.* No, it seems clear that ultimately the boundaries exist for the sake of *enjoying the benefits* of the men, married or otherwise, who do have benefits to offer.

Bill Thrall, a board member and mentor for Leadership Catalyst, speaks often about learning to receive one another's strengths while protecting each other's weaknesses. That's what all this boundary business is really about—protecting weaknesses. My weaknesses. Your weaknesses. Men's weaknesses. Wives' weaknesses. The beauty of this weakness protection plan is that it can free us up to receive (and offer) the available strengths that we and others really do need.

I think of one of my colleagues, Chris. Happily married and the father of five, he is a good, solid man. Together, we work on program, team, and staff development. Chris and I don't delve deeply into one another's private business (and part of my responsibility seems to be to let go of the demand that he know me intimately). But we do have a vulnerable relationship in that each of us seeks to communicate honestly, staying open to the influence of the other. Within this dynamic of our working relationship, I have learned how to do my job better and with greater confidence; his experience and practical knowledge have been strengths I've needed. Likewise, he has gained an appreciation for my ability to analyze and connect relationally. My brain and heart help him do his part better as well.

Recently, we spent four extra hours together in an airport because of weather delays. It wasn't weird. It wasn't bizarre. It was just four extra hours flipping through *People* magazine, eating Balance bars, and making phone calls with Chris sitting—and sometimes snoring—in the chair next to me. Sitting there with the Muzak playing, I felt thankful to have someone next to me. Knowing and trusting that we truly share a common interest (our work), his presence was simply comforting. It was and is almost like having an older brother with me on this leg of the journey.

The benefits of big-brother relationships are not just within a work context. Jana, who is in her late twenties, has experienced something similar in her personal life. "The husband of one of my closest friends from high school is very protective of me. We interact like brother and sister, as we have known each other for over ten years. He once said to me, 'Do not settle for something or someone because you feel like you can't do better.'" This friend's husband was looking out for her, and that was (and is) a benefit Jana cherishes. That "how it is" male perspective, as another woman calls it, is something that a trusted, married, or decidedly unavailable male can offer.

Another friend summed it up well. Men, she said, can support and encourage in "a way that women just can't."

"That's why," as another added, "when I think of the men or women I know who don't get that [opposite sex] contact, I realize how 'unbalanced' they are. Men need to be around women, and women need to be around men."

You probably get the point. As we talked about in chapter 6, we need men—not just potential romances—in our lives. Some relationships do ebb and flow: A friendship with one colleague faded when I left that workplace—it was just too strange to metro downtown for the sole purpose of "catching up" and bantering with a married man. And some need tweaking: Obvious "sparks" with one friend's husband meant my reassessing our one-on-one interaction. And some need some constant reminders: I drop the "My dad and brothers are great!" line frequently around sketchy older men; another friend says "Yes, sir" a lot to keep the wolves at bay. Nevertheless, there is great good to be had in relationships with many of those men who lack romantic potential.

One Friday night, I recounted the contents of this chapter to a friend's boyfriend. Jack replied, "Well, that just sounds like common sense." When he said this, I thought, *Yeah, it does, doesn't it?* I wondered for a moment why I was even bothering to write about it. But simultaneously, I realized that though it *sounds* like common sense, it doesn't *feel* like common sense all the time.

When that small spark ignites for a married man, when that creepy guy gets a little too close, when that work situation demands a level of self-giving that leaves one vulnerable, or when that friend's husband looks at you with the wrong eyes, common sense can quiver and slide. Sure, some women are naturally more tough-minded than others— and most of us could stand to learn from them. But if beneath that tough-mindedness is any kind of malleable heart (which is how I want my heart to be), then clinging to common sense in those moments is key. Actually, sometimes I have to pray that the common sense that my mind possesses would find its way into the strange and powerful corners of my heart.

Recently I read an editorial from *The News & Observer*, a newspaper of Raleigh, North Carolina. Paula Rinehart, a therapist and the editorial's author, reflects on Bill Clinton's memoir, *My Life*, in which he recounts the cost of his "secret life"[43] with a White House intern. She writes:

> Clinton details the parallel between Osama bin Laden's growing threat—and the mounting furor that forced his crisis of publicly coming clean. Indeed, the five days that preceded our best chance to destroy bin Laden and al Qaeda's top staff coincide precisely with the most traumatic personal moments of the President's life—his admission of guilt to his wife and his confession before a grand jury. As Clinton writes, "The American people had to absorb the news of the strike and my

grand jury testimony at the same time." Then on a personal note, he adds, "Hillary and I began a serious counseling program, one day a week for about a year."[44]

Rinehart goes on to explain that any therapist who has worked with a marriage in which there has been betrayal knows that "serious counseling program" is a polite and profoundly understated way of putting it. Such a breach can demand endless hours (even years) of soul-wrenching effort to heal. "As every couple discovers when a partner strays, there is hell to pay."[45]

Common sense? Yeah, it seems like the president and his intern should have had more common sense. Frankly, I wish he'd had the courage of my friend Sarah to just get out of Dodge, to protect his (and his underling's) weaknesses. I bet there could have been incredible and far-reaching benefits. Rinehart adds this observation:

> Unfortunately, this process took place for the Clintons during the time when the threat of al Qaeda and bin Laden was most remediable. . . . Who knows what might have happened if the President had been free to devote his total energy to this gathering storm?[46]

In other words, not respecting the boundaries can rob us—and potentially many others—of untold benefits.

But if presidents and college-educated women can lack common sense, perhaps that means that neither the offices we occupy nor the degrees we tote are guaranteed compasses for any of us. And because it's easy for all of us to get lost in a wilderness (let's face it, the president and his intern just reflect the unboundaried approach to living that our culture celebrates and many of us feel the pull of), we need a reliable compass for the journey.

One morning I was flipping through some stories about Jesus and came across the prayer he prayed the night before he died. One line in it instantly struck me. Praying for those who would follow him, he said, "Father, I want those you have given me to be *with me* where I am, and to see my glory."[47] Immediately, I heard echoes of the question Sandi, the secretary, had asked about my being *with* my boss. Then it dawned on me. The impulse to be *with* another runs strikingly deep. Deep enough that Jesus named it as his eternal desire before he died. Deep enough that fallen men get selfish, wives get jealous, and single women can abuse their capacity to attract. Deep enough to spawn stalkers, gossips, and costly mistakes. The desire to be *with* is strong, and maybe that's why we need those boundaries.

The word *compass* is derived from the Latin words *com* and *passe*, which mean "with" and "pace." Perhaps what we really need, then, is someone to pace, or journey, with. We need a guide to orient us toward the right boundaries—with married men, girlfriends' husbands, old bosses, or whomever—and to be *with* us as we do the work of boundary building. In short, we need a living Compass.

At the risk of sounding obvious, I'm led back again, simply, to the triune God, a God who is presently alive and guides his children. When I survey the scene of relating to men with no romantic potential, when I listen to Celia recount the complexity of her encounters, when I hear my friends' stories, I get a little quiet and my know-it-all impulses chill. I'm just left seeking a greater knowledge and experience of that living Compass.

So in the interim, as I journey, what can I expect? Probably the same as you: big patches of untamed weirdness where the boundaries must be built, and the chance to enjoy, as Cindi says, a harvest of good benefits.

CHAPTER 17

Work Part 1: Good-Bye, Fear

"I don't want to work; I just want to bang on the drum all day. . . ." This refrain from a random eighties song plays through my mind incessantly as I write this chapter. I'm not sure if it's indicative of my current attitude toward having to sit and write when I'd rather be playing (October's bright blue weather beckons me) or if it's simply what characterizes my gut-level response to the word *work*. Tapping my pen like a drumstick on my laptop, I hope it's the former.

Actually, I don't think I am lazy. Except when it comes to keeping my car neat or stopping dust bunny multiplication under my bed, I am like most of the women (married or single) I know: willing to work. But despite this willingness to work hard, among many of my single, childless friends there often lurks a concurrent and fearful ambivalence about work. It is quiet but real, and it sounds something like this: *Am I, by investing myself and my strengths in a career, diminishing the likeli-*

hood that I'll land the job I hope will one day characterize some or all of my adult life—homemaking, motherhood, and greater community life? Conversely, *If I do not invest myself in meaningful work in the present, am I actually sitting on my gifts? Am I missing my opportunity to vigorously make the most of my talents and maybe transform my little piece of the world?*

It isn't a question about the degree to which a woman might pursue paid work outside the home when she's a mother. That's a theoretical question. What's real is that, short of trust funds or lotto earnings, single women must embrace full-time, paid work in order to provide for themselves. If you don't work, you don't eat. So the question for many single women who hope for marriage, family, and/or greater community involvement is this: *How much of myself—my time, my energy, my abilities, my heart—do I give to a career?* *

Rachel, who is in her mid-twenties, came to me not long ago with a question that embodied one side of this tension. Having been in her current mortgage banking position a year and half (and having mastered it to a great degree), she commented:

> I think I'd like to go to law school, but I can't see myself being a full-time lawyer and a wife and mom. If I go to law school, I'll be twenty-seven when I get out, and that would mean not having kids for a few years if I wanted to practice law full-time for a while (which I might also need to do to pay back debt). But that means I'd be old to start as a mom. What do you think?

No doubt about it—Rachel can argue like nobody's business, and she would make an excellent lawyer. And though in my opinion thirty didn't seem terribly old to begin motherhood, I honestly had no idea what would be best for her. In addition to those concerns, she'd also

---

*I've seen my married friends (including men) struggle with this question too—how much to give to their jobs, relative to their families. One twenty-eight-year-old man, Brian, about to get married, mentioned that his father's commitment to financial success had been profitable, and Brian was grateful for the results. But his father's absence had left holes in Brian's life, and Brian wanted to be more available to his wife and children.

spoken to me more than once about men perceiving her strengths as a threat. I had to admit (to myself) that I suspected another degree would simply compound this. And yet was that a valid reason to by-pass law school—to not be a threat? No, it seemed like the best mode of operation was to think in terms not of pleasing an audience of men or well-meaning mentors, but an audience of One. The real question for Rachel was, what might God want from her?

Not long after posing the question, however, Rachel was offered an excellent promotion, so the law school question was put on the back burner. Nevertheless, this new job would bring a higher degree of responsibility, and questions began to bubble about "working longer hours with so many older married people" (presenting challenges about meeting eligible men) as well as the question of relocation (raising issues about community). However, she made her decision to go for it, had a sense of peace, and for now, the next step was settled.

My friend Karen, who's in her thirties, has lived on the flip side of the coin. By her own admission, she has never thought very far ahead, and this has meant paying little attention to the work world.

> I always figured I'd get married and have kids and would want to be around for them. So I guess I've held on to the view that work is this thing passing my time until then. Because of that, I've not really applied myself to finding a job that would be a great fit to help me develop, advance, etc. My mentality has been: This is always temporary. I don't dig in and get a job that fits me well and has potential. Work is this sideline thing I have to do because I'm not married.

For a long time, such an approach worked for Karen. She made friends and money, cared for neighbors, lived abroad, and managed to date a few good men. Life wasn't total suspended animation. But after a recent breakup with a man for whom she had left a job and city in anticipation of marriage, she has begun rethinking things.

> I'm at a place where I want a real job that uses who I am. Not just sitting behind a desk, filling a spot, and making money. It would be awesome to have a job that I could really put my heart into, to use my skills, gifts, leadership, and all that. For the first time in my life, I get really excited about it. I still think that between now and the time I have kids could be a good way off. I don't just want to hang out and not really enter into life. I do think about it now and realize that I need a real job that requires a real me.

So for now, that's the direction Karen is headed. She knows that if she lands such a job, and if things reignite with her ex-boyfriend or someone else, she might have to make choices that she could have otherwise avoided. But for today, the desire to engage in a real job that requires a real self (which, as an aside, is the kind of self she'd like to take into marriage and family as well) is—in conjunction with a sense of God's leading—shaping her next steps.

The career-marriage question is not an easy one to answer. At what point is waiting and holding oneself back a worthy step toward creating space not just for men or marriage but also for friendships, extended family, hobbies, service, community, and spontaneity? And at what point is that self-restraint simply fear expressing itself in passivity or strategic attempts to manipulate future outcomes? Perhaps few of us can make that judgment from a single glance. Even when it comes to ourselves, sometimes motives are hard to see.

When I was working at the international public policy think tank, I couldn't understand myself relative to the whole work thing. I'd burned out on doing people-helping-nonprofit-underdog things; they had left me feeling poor and stressed. I'd wanted a knight to rescue me, and none had. Therefore I'd leaped at the chance to land in a stable, reputable, marble-and-chrome-lobbied downtown office. It paid better, and the stress—an initially steep learning curve—was offset by the free Starbucks coffee, private office, and great location. Maybe for me it was selling out, but that seemed better than any visible alternative.

Then one day my boss, a delightful Brit with a way of slicing through the muck of fuzzy thoughts, looked at me during my review and challenged me in his charming and pointed way. "Connally, if you could really learn the content of a few program areas—like issues of the economy in South Asia, for example—you could really go places here. And if you don't want to do that sort of thing, you might need to ask yourself what, in fact, you really do want."

How about a handsome husband and a cool house? I wanted to, but didn't, reply. Actually, my desires were no secret to anybody, but owning them hadn't brought about their realization. So now the question was staring me in my face (a great grace, in retrospect), and it was time to face reality. Honestly, I knew I'd rather be shot and hung than seriously learn about the economy of South Asia—no offense to those who have a very legitimate passion for this subject. No matter how hard I tried to pretend, I didn't care beyond five o'clock about international public policy—actually, I barely made it that far. So what in the world was I doing in a job that required that passion?

Strangely enough, this discussion happened about the same time as a weekend visit home for my father's sixtieth birthday party. It was a fancy ordeal, complete with out-of-town guests. Late Saturday night, after the festivities had ended, my aunt Bonnie and I stood in the guest bathroom, taking off our makeup, chatting. Slowly, our conversation morphed into one of those talks about the meaning of life. As I shared some of my work struggles, she wiped a cotton ball around her eye and said—as if it were the most obvious thing in the world—"You know, it sounds like you're Jonah, and you've been running away from what God wants you to do. And now, honey, you've gotten yourself stuck in the belly of the whale."

I guess some people *can* judge accurately in a glance.

So what does a woman do when her British boss and her aunt Bonnie from Texas, whom she barely ever sees, can smell her issues a mile away? when she realizes that, like the servant who hid his talent in the ground for fear that the master was a tyrant,[48] she too has buried her talents for fear that God is perhaps a little twisted? when she faces her suspicion that God is someone who might give her gifts in communication, spiritual leadership, and vision that, if she were to use them fully, would sabotage the very desires of her heart for marriage and possibly a family? (The fear wasn't totally irrational. Try plugging those attributes into a Match.com profile. While they might earn respect, they are not usually men magnets.) What does a woman do when she realizes that, like Jonah, her attempts at under-the-radar strategizing to get what she wants have landed her in the dark and dank belly of a whale?

In short, she does something that people have been doing for thousands of years: She repents. *Repent.* That word is rarely heard except in TV shows or comic books. Or picture the crazy man wearing a "Repent!" placard as he wanders New York City streets. It is a word that can leave anyone squirming (does repentance lead to dressing in Bible verse placards and standing on corners with megaphones?). But repent is what she does. That's what I did.

Sitting behind my computer in my windowless office, staring at unfiled papers and a keyboard with dust in its crevices, I repented. *God, I've buried the talents you've given me because I've feared how my life might go if I use them. I've been wrong. Please forgive me.* Then—hoping no one would barge into my office while tears dribbled onto my keyboard, I laid that whole big pile of strengths and weaknesses, dreams and fears, down before him. *Okay, God, my talents—and my desires—are yours. You gave them to me; now I'm giving them back to you, for you to do with them what you'd like. No more ineffective strategic hoarding and stingy distribution for my own purposes.*

In response, I wasn't suddenly shot out of the whale's belly. But something shifted. My relentless need to control my future was broken, a crack emerged in the status quo, and slowly the whale's mouth opened. With a great deal of messy freedom—crawling through whale guts is never pretty—I began the climb out.

Of course, my personal story of talent-smushing isn't universal for all single women. I smile now when I think of my friends whose struggles have never been sitting on their talents out of a desire to get a husband or a certain life. My Southern sister-in-law, Vicki, had visions of busting into the political scene in Washington, DC, and she jumped in with her twenty-two-year-old Alabama guns a-blazin'. She has now taken that same drive into her overseas life as a—first corporate and then missionary—wife and mother. Or I think of my friend Jen, who knows what she is good at, searches out opportunities, and in a fistful of years since college, has taken incredible risks to use her gifts. I've envied that spirit of engagement with her work. Neither of these women seems to struggle with talent-smushing.

Perhaps, though, whether we're talent smushers or talent celebrators or somewhere in between, finding the answer to the question, How much of myself—my time, my energy, my abilities, my heart— do I give to a career? begins at the same place for all of us: acknowledging that we can't control an unpredictable work or relational future. We can only face what's real in the present, offer our talents back up to the Talent Giver, and move forward with the best wisdom we have. (There's a bit more on the wisdom piece in the next chapter.)

One weekend I was at a friend's wedding. Seated next to me at the reception was a woman who worked in recruiting for the armed forces. As you might guess, this topic of women and work came up in our discussion. It turns out she had attended the Naval Academy in Annapolis. During her time there, she'd decided not to pursue naval aviation—her desire and something for which she was gifted—because it would have been a ten-year commitment. She knew she wanted to marry and have children, so with that in mind, though there was no husband on the horizon, she chose another route.

As it turned out, she didn't marry until she was thirty-four—twelve years after she graduated—which would have been plenty of time to fulfill an aviator's commitment. I asked how she looked at her vocational decision making in retrospect. A thoughtful woman who often fielded questions like these from female recruits, she admitted that she had sat upon her aviator talents out of both fear and other desires. She had wanted to give God the biggest amount of space possible to work a husband into her life, her biggest desire. But, she reminded me, there is a fine line between giving God space to work in certain ways and demanding, if ever so subtly, that he work in the ways we envision. In retrospect, she admitted that she had crossed that line.

Her advice now to a younger woman entering the military is simply to make the best decision you can with what you know now. The future is not guaranteed, so—while holding on to your job and family desires alike—work with the choices presently available to you. Then leave the outcome to God.

In her words I heard echoes of Karen's yearning to engage real work with her real self, trusting God with the rest. I heard echoes of my own experiences. And I heard echoes of the story of the master and the servant. *Make the most of your talents, and trust God with the rest.* These words ring true.

This would be an apt place to end this chapter, but I'd be remiss if I failed to mention one other point. Most of the people I know, myself included, haven't done so well with *trusting God with the rest.* Many of my friends and I find trusting, in one area of life if not another, tough. One twenty-three-year-old woman, when trying to decide between getting another job in DC and moving back home to Iowa, said, "I feel like I'm standing on a tall column in a sea of fog. If I misstep, I will plummet to some unseen valley far below." But that's when a smile creeps back over my face. What I've discovered is that the Talent Giver isn't twisted; he is gracious. His response to both our repentance over our foolish failings and our regret over our earnest missteps is surprising. Our messed-up views of ourselves or him, our misused talents in work or life, and our quiet line-crossing do not elicit harshness. Instead, he forgives at a cost to himself, draws us near, and beckons us to continue *with him*. Somehow he turns our mistakes—our stumbling blocks—into stepping-stones for the journey forward. Foggy and fearful concern about over- or under-giving to our careers need not haunt us. Rather, we're set free to do the best we can with what we have and grow to trust God with the rest. And while it might feel like we're standing on a tall pillar in a sea of fog, as we can learn to trust, we'll eventually discover the solid ground beneath us, which rises up to meet us, even as we leap.

CHAPTER 18

Work Part 2: Hello, Wisdom

Perhaps a discussion about how much of oneself to give to a career is the prerogative of the Western educated leisure class. When I was researching for this chapter, one African-American friend, Maria, reminded me, "It's a privilege to dream about doing what you like or desire." She said, "It's been ingrained in us as a people that you're not always going to enjoy what you do, but you do it because that's what it takes to survive. You have to deal with and find contentment in your current reality. Then you can dream." Her point is fair. There are numerous women of many colors who have unimaginable constraints in life, and they live, work, and die within these constraints. How can one have anything but respect for those who've marched on, never having the chance to realize their dreams? And though sometimes comments like Maria's bring me up short, I am thankful when she and others remind me to be humbly grateful for what might be called the problems of privilege.

These dilemmas, though, are where many of us live. There are more well-educated single women of all backgrounds marching into the professional work world—and staying there longer—than ever before. Vocational opportunities, though not boundless or distributed equally, are abundant. And we bear the uneasy responsibility of deciding how we'll proceed. So the question inevitably presents itself to a greater number of women: *I have talents, and I want to use them well and wisely in my lifetime, plus support myself in the process. . . . How do I do it?*

Think of that famous career self-help book *What Color Is Your Parachute?* In endless editions since 1970, it has sold over 8 million copies. I couldn't touch that type of insight and influence if I wanted to! Still, I have lived much longer with this single woman/work thing than I ever intended. Some people are married to their work. For me, work is more like a distant, older uncle who came to visit for a year and has stayed with me for fifteen. Though he's always been a bit quirky and inscrutable, we've gotten to know—and even appreciate—each other over the years. So I now have a few insights into him that just might help you, however you may be related to him.

I've listened—informally and in interviews—to many friends and acquaintances on the topic of work. My unscientific conclusion is that the ones who derive the greatest satisfaction from their work are not those who are paid the most (though nobody mentioned a problematically high salary) or even those who are the most powerful (though a few did mention the stress of too much responsibility). Rather, those who are most satisfied are those who are using their strengths* for something or someone greater than themselves.

Put in the inverse: Making work first and foremost about my self-actualization, my self-aggrandizement, or my plain old profit is ulti-

---

*Interestingly, Leslie Martin, president of the Highlands Consulting Group and an executive coach, notes that it's normally the presence of unused abilities rather than overused abilities that generates job dissatisfaction.

mately a dead end. Perhaps it seems crazy. If I sit fearfully on my talents, I'm a goner. But if I pick them up, own them, and exercise them for nothing greater than my personal gain, eventually something in me will wilt, or even die. (As an aside, perhaps that's why the prospect of provision for a loved one can motivate those whose vocational dreams have been tabled. While the actual work they do might lack personal meaning, there is still a greater purpose to their labor.)

With some of the single men I've known, this wilting manifests itself more obviously than with their female counterparts. For many guys, with neither wives nor kids to care for and with jobs that offer money but don't invite attachment to a bigger purpose, their lives degenerate into gadget getting—wider screens for their TVs or cooler cars for their garages. Meanwhile, their energies to engage with life meaningfully seem to seep away; their souls get stuck in cul-de-sacs.

In the 1999 tongue-in-cheek cult classic movie *Office Space*, Peter, the twenty-eight-year-old corporate computer programmer, bemoans, "Ever since I started working, every single day of my life has been worse than the day before it. So that means that every single day that you see me, that's on the worst day of my life." The caricatured, Dilbert-esque monotony of his job is kind of funny, in a pitiful way. The guy is making money, but he is definitely wilting.

Before he's a complete zombie, though, Peter finally finds it within himself to push back—he knocks down his cubicle to gangsta rap, defies his insipid boss, and stops showing up. In his own way, he's beating back the system that's sucking his life away. About the same time, he also meets a woman. As their relationship grows, he tells her, "I may never be happy in my job, but I think that if I could be with you, I could be happy with my life." It's a small start, but Peter has now found a *purpose* for working: to eat so he can stay alive and be with his girlfriend. With that platform underneath him, Peter takes a new job that uses his strengths (construction) and is coming home happy to this woman.

Okay, so Peter from *Office Space* isn't a contemporary superhero. But this movie reflects some of the same things I've been seeing: People long to use their abilities for something of greater value than themselves. Women (single or married) are no exception.

What does seem a bit different for many of the women I've engaged with regarding this topic is *what* is considered valuable. At the risk of making a grotesque gender generalization (I can imagine a few dear friends furrowing their eyebrows in disagreement), it seems that most women value depth and breadth in relationships more than most men do. In my observations, this orientation seems to make the vocation question a bit more complex for many women. Had *Peter* actually been *Penelope*, my guess is that the movie would have played out differently.

For example, women oftentimes—for better and for worse—seem to invest in and draw more life from their workplace relationships than men do. Hence, a woman's actual job might be a misfit—one that doesn't engage her best abilities—but she'll stay in it longer for the sake of the people. Or sometimes, because she is so oriented toward connecting, she may even get angry with colleagues when they don't behave like a husband or family—though colleagues generally lack a covenantal or blood relationship with one another. Conversely, she may be an absolutely excellent department manager, but she feels the ache and pull for marriage, family, or more solid friendships than her male counterpart does. And that can create a distinct internal struggle.

Maybe this complexity around what is perceived as valuable is why there's angst surrounding the questions—real or potential—about paid career versus unpaid motherhood (or community life). In both spheres there are legitimate and important opportunities to use one's God-given abilities for something or someone(s) greater than oneself. This is a wonderful privilege, but it can confuse a person. Perhaps that's why the way to proceed is to do as that recruiter suggested and simply make the wisest choice given the available options.

That might be easier said than done, however. Making wise vocational choices can be tough. Often we aren't sure about our abilities, and sometimes it's hard to get beyond ourselves in our thinking.* Still, there are ways to gain wisdom in this area. Author Frederick Buechner gives a helpful rule of thumb for moving forward. He writes:

> The kind of work God usually calls you to is the kind of work (a) that you need most to do and (b) that the world most needs to have done. If you really get a kick out of your work, you've presumably met requirement (a), but if your work is writing TV deodorant commercials, the chances are you've missed requirement (b). On the other hand, if your work is being a doctor in a leper colony, you have probably met requirement (b), but if most of the time you're bored and depressed by it, the chances are you have not only bypassed (a) but probably aren't helping your patients much either. . . . The place God calls you to is the place where your deep gladness and the world's deep hunger meet.[49]

Buechner's advice, of course, presupposes that we know what brings us gladness and we know about important needs beyond our own. And for many, discovering these things is work in and of itself. You might stop right now and ask yourself, *What brings me gladness?* and

*I've wondered, too, if for some single women (this is my issue, but I don't think I'm alone), a failure to think in terms "beyond ourselves" actually messes up our thoughts about men, motherhood, and our futures. When my vision of marriage and/or family telescopes solely into a focus on filling my own emotional needs, I can easily begin to develop a weird and unhelpful mental dichotomy between "working" and "having a family." I can almost see the responsibility to engage my abilities for something greater than myself as something from which a husband and family will rescue me. *Finally, I won't have to work, but I'll just be filled!* But when I listen to both stay-at-home moms and those who work outside the home, even the ones who are deeply fulfilled in family life admit that marriage and family development require considerable work and don't meet their every soul need. If we're fundamentally looking to get rescued "out of work" and land in consummate nirvana, we'll ultimately be disappointed, whether we're looking to the lottery or our love lives.

What is more important than I am? Both are worth considering. As you do, you might also discover that the intersection between one's gladness and the world's hunger can manifest itself in a myriad of callings.

I've seen this gladness for Carol in public service, first through government work and then in consulting. Cheryl finds herself called for now to serve as a vice president of a national faith-based organization that needs her gifts. Maria values the chance to help heal others through massage; Abby loves to see middle schoolers think and write. Mary Ellen raises children full-time; Polly raises money for higher education but hopes to switch into raising a child. And Kristen finds a deep gladness in doing her law job well but also having enough mental and emotional time to be available for friends. The gladness-hunger combinations are as varied and fluid as the women God has created.

Such variety brings its own challenges. The lessening of constraints and the presence of so many possibilities can paralyze those of us who don't have razor-sharp vocational vision. Perhaps as we talk of using our talents for something greater than ourselves, we need to take a still more essential step—beyond gladness and hunger identification—to gain wisdom. Our English word *vocation* comes from the Latin word *vocare*, which means "to call."[50] Perhaps our foundational task in vocation discovery is learning to hear and respond to the voice of the Caller, i.e., the triune God.

This is not as impractical or as out-there as it might initially sound. If the Caller is real—if there is in fact a God who calls us to places— we can reasonably expect that he knows whom he's calling. And if he knows us, it seems safe to conclude that he has insights into our talents and the world in which we use them. Isn't it likely, then, that in learning to hear and respond to his voice, we'll learn to engage with the work world—as teachers, lawyers, mothers, administrators, or some combo platter—more wisely? Solomon, the wise and ancient king of Israel, knew this need for the Caller's wisdom. He wrote:

> If you call out for insight and cry aloud for understanding, and if you look for it as for silver and search for it as for hidden treasure, then you will understand the fear of the LORD and find the knowledge of God. For the LORD gives wisdom, and from his mouth come knowledge and understanding. . . . Then you will understand what is right and just and fair—every good path. For wisdom will enter your heart, and knowledge will be pleasant to your soul.[51]

A right, just, fair—and good—path. Isn't that the kind of path you'd like to follow into your vocational future, even if it is into unknown territory? And whether that path eventually leads to the top of a corporate ladder, the basement with a laundry basket, or most likely, somewhere in-between, don't you want to be fundamentally pleased with the destination *and* the journey? I thirst for such life-giving and soul-pleasing wisdom to fill my heart now and into the future, whatever my work.

I mentioned previously that at my think tank job I had grown tired of functioning like a Peter-esque nine-to-fiver. My strategizing had landed me in a dead end: a misfit job, no husband, little gladness, and shaky purpose. What I perhaps failed to mention was that during that time, I had finally begun crying out to the Caller, beseeching the one who had bestowed my gifts. Really, pain has a way of humbling me (it's a shame humility doesn't come more naturally). So I was begging God: *Help me! I'll stay here if you want.* Many of the people were wonderful, and the pay wasn't bad. *But show me what to do.* My heart's yearning for more kept bubbling up, no matter how many hip happy hours I went to.

Finally that yearning relentlessly rushed in on me during one work-related conversation. It was like water suddenly gushing into the cracks of the status quo (cracks caused by my boss's question, "What do you want?" and my aunt's observation of my whale-belly living). I was meeting with a woman from a major foundation to discuss funding for our Soviet Studies program. As we talked, the conversation kept drifting toward her recent struggles. I found myself wanting to understand her, to know what she was thinking, to see what she was really after. Her pauses and faraway looks seemed significant, and it took all my power to sit on my impulses and keep the conversation on track. My company was not paying me to spiritually guide potential funders. By our conversation's end, it was clear. The work I needed to do—my deep gladness—would always be addressing people's spiritual hunger.

Whose hunger and in what way were not clear. But what was clear was that the Caller was at work. He was beckoning me to take the next step. Encouraged by the people who knew me well, I decided to respond. In my own version of playing Peter in *Office Space*, I decided to push back. But instead of knocking down my cubicle and defying my boss (I had a cool office and a great boss), my push back looked like taking risks—the risks of admitting what made me glad, owning what needs I observed in God's world, and discovering the path to bring the two together, for a salary.

So here I am, five years later, working on staff for a faith-based organization, really liking most of what I do. I'm not (yet) married, and so—as a sideline—I'm writing this book on God-sightings in the context of unintentional singleness. Go figure. If I had had my druthers, my steps out of the whale's belly would have led not to writing this book but instead to giving speeches about handling my rich, hot husband's chronic attention to the details of my heart while managing, together, our exceptionally talented children, our world-changing ideas, and our important community activities. Fantasy does die hard. But that's not the work I've presently been called to (and most likely, it's not a monologue for which any segment of the world is hungering). So for now I rest content in my calling but with my eyes glancing toward the horizon.

It might at this point be easy to think, *Oh, this chick does religious work.* *Of course that's a calling. But that's not me. I like accounting or business or event planning or . . .* Nope. I've spoken to too many other women (and men) who possess a strong sense of calling or vocation that is not religious in nature. My friend Elizabeth always envisioned herself working to make an inner-city, mom-and-pop, nonprofit organization soar. It took her a long time to realize, however, that her gifts and gladness were far more suited to bringing administrative order to a large, bustling, profitable organization. Letting go of her vision of where she "should" be was hard. But as she's searched out God's wisdom and sought to understand more of her abilities and the world's needs, she has been led to embrace work in just such an organization. She's trusting that her commitment to excellence and to bringing the transforming presence of Jesus to her office and work is a significant (if not her only) calling.

Do you find yourself wishing that *vocation discovery* were an instant or at least a linear process? How great would it be to plug the following steps into our Palm pilots and then check them off as they are finished: *This week: (1) Meet the Caller, (2) Hear his words,* and *(3) Discover my talents. Next week: (1) Understand the world's great needs, (2) Gladly meet those hungers,* and *(3) Make some money.* Perhaps we could also add, *Buy cool, sassy black skirt to wear to work; Find perfect coffee mug for desk;* and *Get excellent job title that plays well at parties.* Maybe it does happen systematically for some women, but for 95 percent of the ones I know, it doesn't. Sometimes we make some money, buy our dream things, and discover, "Whoa, I'm still not happy." Sometimes we have a phenomenal spiritual revelation on Sunday but dread Monday through Friday's job of selling handbags, yet we have to eat. Sometimes we know we're a hot commodity, but we never get the recognition we merit. Whatever our lingering need—direction, gladness, money, whatever—it pushes and pulls us, and the discovery process continues.

It's a journey, no doubt. But what those who've gone before me

keep telling me (and my experience agrees) is that as we seek the
Caller en route, a clearer picture of our vocation—how best to gladly
use our abilities to satisfy hungers beyond our own—slowly emerges.
We grow increasingly aware of *what is right and just and fair—every good
path*. We gradually learn how to use our talents well and wisely in our
lifetime, plus support ourselves in the process. In short, we learn
something about living with the uncle I mentioned at the outset—the
one who inevitably lives with all of us in some form or fashion. And as
wisdom enters and shapes our hearts and choices, we might even
learn what it is to humbly and gratefully love the old guy.

CHAPTER 19

Where's the Village?

There is a longing in my heart not just for personal wholeness and oneness with a husband but also for being woven into a community of people whose whole is greater than the sum of the parts, whose purpose is bigger than itself. And I yearn for this to be with people who, as my friend Anne says, "are willing to need one another and meet one another's needs . . . people who share a kind of collective ownership of one another."

I suspect that these longings and aches are not unique to me. I'd venture to guess that to different degrees, they are present in the souls of almost everyone. But for single women living in the West—perhaps because we generally are relational creatures living independent lives by choice or necessity—questions about community relentlessly clamor for an answer.

The question I hear over and over again from my single friends, particularly as they move into and beyond their late twenties, is basic:

Where can I find community? It's as if the aloneness of single life—taking your car to the mechanic yourself, buying zucchini for one—intrinsically highlights questions about being connected to others. When I was in graduate school, I read an essay by poet Michael Ryan. In it, he talked about two contrary pulls in the human heart: one toward independence and the other toward connection. He called this latter pull the desire for *seamlessness*.[52] Many of my friends experience life as a patchwork of piecemeal relationships with potential to unravel, yet most of us yearn to be seamlessly woven into a rich tapestry of others.

So, where is community found? Former first lady Hillary Clinton made famous the phrase, "It takes a village to raise a child." I couldn't agree more. Communities of folks with a degree of interdependence and shared commitment are necessary for raising children *and* for sustaining adults. As the poet John Donne wrote, "No man is an island." But with all due respect to first ladies and famous poets, I'm just wondering—and perhaps you've wondered too—*where do I find the village?* Is it found with colleagues? scattered family members? church friends? sports teams? neighbors? some combination of all the above? It's not always easy to know where to look.

Surveying a variety of friends, I found that community is hard to come by for many single women, or at least hard to hold on to. "I'm on my third set of friends right now," writes one woman who has cycled through the marriages and moves of numerous friends. Says another woman, Sarah:

> Growing up in a small town, I was surrounded by folks who were very supportive and provided lots of encouragement. . . . My city experiences have been a bit different. Although I have had good friends, it seems like folks are more willing to let you go it alone; you are on their radar screen if it looks like you are in dire need somehow, but on a day-to-day basis you make life work on your own.

It seems that the greatest communal constant for many single women is their girlfriends. Sarah continues, "I have had close girlfriends who do not fit this mold; they were/are much more caring about successes (both personal and professional), and these women have been single and married alike." Karen, who is Japanese-American, has also found community with Japanese girlfriends in the area. "I feel a sense of belonging, though I'm not exactly like them. I feel as if I'm accepted for who I am and can connect with them at a deep level."

But as great as the sisterhood can be, I don't think it's quite enough to constitute community in the fullest sense. Fuller community seems to include, at least ideally, a variety of families, toddlers, teenagers, and old people. Says Sarah, "This [kind of diversity] reminds me of the community I grew up in and find to be the most life-giving. . . . It's a way in which I can get beyond thinking about the issues of my small life and be concerned about others' lives and the good times—or not-so-good times—they experience." My friend Laurie also has experienced the joy of rubbing up against a variety of people within her church:

> Seeing the lives of the people who make up the church,
> especially the older married couples and families . . . adds a
> deep dimension to my vision and spiritual mentorship. . . .
> I trust them from watching them every week. My history
> here is a sense of rootedness that is rich for me. . . .
> [Specifically,] Sal and Tim and their family are a home for me
> emotionally.

There is something about this multilayered interconnectedness with others that epitomizes a sense of community. This is how Libby describes her vision for the future: "My dream is that if I am elderly and single . . . people will drop by my house a lot, and I will be often at my friends' families' homes—without needing appointments for either . . . that there will be a feeling of safety, comfort, and familiarity."

Hmm, I think to myself, *that's what I want too—to be woven into a colorful, seamless community blanket.* It's just not always easy to come by. Much has been written about the national breakdown of our sense of common identity. As one famous book put it, people just aren't bowling together anymore.[53] If we're not bowling together, and if we're moving a lot, shared history is hard to develop. But in all fairness, I'm wondering if the problem isn't just "them"—all those non-bowling, transient people out there messing up community and leaving me isolated. I'm seeing that I might have a part in this community thing too.

I entered adulthood presuming that community—be it one centered around a similar vision of faith or one centered around shared civic interests or, ideally, a little of both—would just be there for me. There was supposed to be some village out there, some pool of people waiting for you or me (and my presumed husband) to dive in and make a life with them. I think of a hypothetical man whose vision for his future was shaped by his stay-at-home mom, who had done his laundry, cooked his meals, and entertained his father's colleagues. How shocked would this man be to realize that the woman he had now married expected him to make his own breakfast or launder his own shirts? The paradigm on which he had built his sense of self and vision would be missing, and he'd feel lost (and perhaps a little upset).

So what might be reasonable to expect of such a man? Maybe that he'd learn to scramble eggs or iron clothes. Maybe that he'd join his wife in examining their mutual expectations of marriage. Maybe they'd have to work together in ways neither of them was familiar with. Both husband and wife would have to become learners.

Shoot. Sometimes I wish life didn't take so much learning. I'd like to sail on the track already laid out by previous generations. My mom said to me recently, "Your generation spends so much time having to analyze and define everything—when do you get to just live?" I looked at her like, *Hello! Sorry! We're not the ones who blew the tracks to smithereens.* We have to lay new track in order to move forward. That's just reality.

What I've realized is that I have to become a learner in terms of community. Frankly, I hate being remedial. That's why I've put off learning this lesson for as long as I could. Part of me has always banked on holding my breath long enough for the husband to come through, trusting that then the community would emerge from the mist—a living Camelot of sorts—to receive us.

Snap. Reality check. Unfortunately, I think I'm the one who has been in the fog. And when I look around, I see I'm in the beginner's class. At least that's what it feels like given my single, urban, transient context. I'm a girl whose "home" phone is a little black cell phone that is easily left behind at the airport in Austin or Albuquerque. I'm a girl whose most permanent address is @some-server-in-cyberspace (what is a server, anyhow?). But at least I'm becoming a girl who is willing to learn. And this is what I have been learning.

Lesson number one: The village might not exist, or at least not in the way you or I envision it. Lesson number two: You and I might have to help build (or rebuild) the village. My roommate has one of those cool, square-shaped greeting cards posted on our fridge. The hip-lettering-on-black-background quote, attributed to Gandhi, reads: "Be the change you wish to see in the world." Okay, I don't exactly know what it means to *be the village* (reminds me of a tennis coach I had who used to say, "Be the ball"—I didn't know what that meant, either). But I am learning something about laying bricks and mortar, so to speak, even as a single woman in a shifting culture.

Truth and love, I am convinced, are the bricks and mortar of building any kind of community. Without one, you end up with a big, oozed-out pile of useless cement. Without the other, you end up with a jagged, fragile, and dangerous structure. I'd venture to say that at some point all of us have experienced hard-core truth that has wounded us and soggy love that has kept us stuck. One without the other is no good.

But what might it take to hold truth and love together? This sounds basic—I am a beginner, you know—but I'm learning that it starts with believing that each actually exists. Most people I know are loath, at least publicly, to call anything *universally true*. We might trust that our feelings about something are true for us, e.g., *I love high heels* or *I can't stand [fill-in-the-blank] people*, but saying, *Yep, there's stuff that's absolutely true, regardless of my feelings* sends shivers up many people's spines. It even makes me twitch, and I actually believe in the existence of absolute truth. But imagine trying to build a community without any definitive truth. It would be like trying to conduct a symphony without the assurance that notes, scales, and chords could be counted on to have a reliable, repeatable, universal pitch. Can you imagine how tough symphony building would be if that were the case?

Likewise, believing that love isn't just "a secondhand emotion," as Tina Turner puts it, is also key. I don't know about you, but I see in myself and many folks around me the secret suspicion that love, except for perhaps romantic love that's rarely fleshed out beyond sex, actually doesn't exist. It's just hard for many of us to trust that real love from fathers to daughters, girlfriends to girlfriends, or leaders to followers really is out there. After you've been disappointed, it feels safer to assume an agenda and be proven wrong, rather than the reverse. If real, self-giving, others-centered love is not possible, why would anyone risk connecting with imperfect people who will inevitably mess you up?

But assume with me, if you can, that true Truth and real Love are out there and we can know them, at least in part. (My presupposition is that they are lodged in and an extension of a true and loving triune God.) How could we embody them in some kind of a community? How could we build them into some kind of village, given our early twenty-first-century urban Western realities?

I've seen the shadows of blueprints in a few real-life scenarios.

Kristi, a single woman who works full-time as a counselor and offici-
ates basketball games on the side, writes:

> I probably experience [community] right now in my small
> cohort from officiating. . . . We are close because we know
> that when we walk out onto the floor, nobody else in the
> arena likes us. Any decision we make always angers a group of
> people, including players, coaches, and fans. Thus, we learn to
> trust and depend on each other.

There is something about a shared sense of purpose that creates a
need for interdependence. Interdependence, which presumes a
level of trust, in turn seems to bind people together. When I lived in
inner-city Philly, late one summer night my roommates and I heard
the rumblings of a crowd of people outside. Hesitantly we opened
the door to see a group of thirty or forty middle-aged and elderly
people, waving flashlights and sporting caps with an insignia I now
forget. They were chanting defiantly, "Drug dealers go home! Drug
dealers go home!" As we talked with them, they explained that they
were tired of watching their neighborhood die. And while no one
person was a match for the dealers, maybe together they could do
something to help.

A deeply shared sense of mission doesn't just *draw* people together,
however. It can also create a reason to *stick* together—to work
through differences, to forgive one another. Recently I was at a meeting for work where the original agenda was flipped on its head. Why?
The two primary factions represented had seriously bad blood between them. As I sat through two days of hair-pulling discussions,
part of me wanted to scream, "Oh please, can we just get on with the
agenda?" But as time passed, and as the offenses like splinters were
drawn out and healed by the poultice of apology and forgiveness, I
observed something: *Without a compelling sense of purpose, nothing would*

make the excruciating work of reconciliation worth the effort. And without reconcili-
ation, this motley group would ultimately unravel. But in this instance, reconciliation was happening, and a sense of authentic community was
deepening. Frankly, it amazed me and gave me hope.

Still, at the end of the day, maybe basketball officiating, neighborhood street marches, mission organizations, or historic bonds with
local congregations aren't in your immediate grasp. Maybe you're like
a friend of mine whose profound sense of purpose—I'd go so far as to
say *call*—necessitates so much travel that her community, such as it is,
is scattered internationally. But she still needs some sense of home
base. Or maybe you're honestly confused about what your purpose is,
let alone how it fits with others' callings, so it's hard to lock onto some
shared mission with any integrity. My friend Phil is genuinely trying
to answer the "What am I here for" question, but still he yearns for
community right now. It might be too neat and unrealistic a package
to simply say, "Get your purpose—find your core people and work
through the junk to keep the community hopping" (though that
would be nice). So some of us who are in the beginner's class have to
start a little smaller, trusting that eventually, as an ancient prophet
once declared, "the least of you [even us?] will become a thousand,
the smallest a mighty nation."[54]

When my friend Anne said community is about people who "need
one another and meet one another's needs," I think she also was hint-
ing at blueprints for building at least a mini-village. I suspect that historically needs were more obvious—I need your help to gather my
crops; you need my help to ward off invaders. I need your help to raise
my child; you need my help to raise your barn. But now we have to
work a little harder at even knowing, let alone revealing, our needs—
needs that are often less tangible or visible but just as real.

Maybe village building starts with laying down a straight and
honest verbal brick, such as "I'm a little lonely and was wondering if
you'd eat dinner and hang out with me tonight" and waiting, a bit ex-

posed, for someone to lay down the cement of "Sure." Or instead of
walking away at the first dropped brick, it's admitting, "Ouch, that
seriously hurt"—and being willing to forgive. I remember one colleague who made some off-the-cuff comment about my being
thirty-four, unmarried, and not sleeping with anyone. "Maybe you
like girls?" he joked. Because I'd trusted him enough to be honest
about my sleeping habits, his words stung. So the next day I mus-
tered up the courage to say, "Eric, you know your comment yesterday—it stung." I explained why: Staying celibate without desexing
yourself is hard, especially when you're seen as, at best, a sweet
anachronism. In this vulnerable arena, I needed his help, not his humor. He heard me and ended up apologizing profusely. Admittedly,
he did not understand me (he had three categories: married, sleeping with your boyfriend, or gay—and I fit none), but he really didn't
mean to hurt me. Such as it was, our tiny workplace village was pre-
served through that small exchange.

Or maybe the risky brick we set down is lovingly speaking truth
not just about ourselves but directly to others. One rainy night when I
wanted to go downtown and take ice cream to this man I'd been seeing, my roommate Paula tried to talk me out of it. "It's too late," she
said, noting the 9:30 time. "It'll be dangerous walking to his office
building." But I had pepper spray on my key chain and a great um-
brella. She tried a few more approaches, and then she threw up her
hands. "Maria," she yelled, "come talk to this woman; she's insane." In
walked my other roommate, Maria, who looked me straight in my
eyeballs. I will never forget what she said: "Girl, if he's actually working late, it's because he's actually working. If you go downtown to see
him, one of three things will happen. One, he won't be there, and
you'll be confused and wondering. Two, he will be there, will be
working, and won't have time for a distraction. Or three, he'll be
alone in that office and you know what distraction you'll both be interested in." She studied me. "Girl, if somewhere in the back of your

mind you're thinking *booty call*, you'd better sit your butt down on this bed and go nowhere until morning, or you'll regret it."

Like a child caught red-handed, I looked away, but a faint grin spread across my face. "Busted," I said, and smiled at being known—and cared for—enough by Paula and Maria to have my weaknesses protected. I stayed put, and the bond between my roommates and me deepened.

You get the idea. We exchange with one another the bricks and cement of truth and love. Maybe then we go a little further, expanding our circles and saying to that fun couple with small kids, "Could we commit to getting together twice a month for dinner?" It's awkward and it might be a bust, but it's worth it. Or maybe it's just picking a faith-based community group, committing to meet with them for a year, and seeing what happens. I tried it, and three years later there's a restful, solid bond among us.

There is something about simply making commitments. My friend Kristie is married to Paul, but she still longs for that *village*. In seeking it, she has discovered that her "most powerful experiences of community . . . are within the context of committed relationships" (including but not limited to marriage). Her moments of intentionally "speaking those words of commitment to one another" have made all the difference. "Suddenly you begin to act differently toward each other. You want to heal wounds; you are much more careful not to offend or hurt."

Speaking of hurt, there is the virtual guarantee that you and I will, in spite of (or because of) our shared vulnerability, purpose, and commitment, get hurt. If you commit to village building, inevitably a brick will drop on your foot or the cement will dry in your hair. You will lovingly stick it out there, as a friend of mine says, and get it chopped off. Reconciliation and/or healing will be needed at some point. But this is where trusting in the real existence of a loving, triune God is crucial for a few reasons.

"Unless the LORD builds the house, those who build it labor in vain,"[55] declared the wise poet-king Solomon. Perhaps we need a real and loving God not just to give us specs for village building but also to be present with us throughout our inevitable labor pains. Maybe it's his grace that can undergird and enable the crucial work of forgiving—and replacing—dropped bricks or sloppy cement. Without it, our attempts might be in vain. With it, hope is real.

Of course, willingness to rely on God's help depends on believing that God actually yearns to be in this whole village building thing with us. That's a faith gamble, but I think it's a good bet. If the Father, Son, and Holy Spirit live together in some kind of divinely mysterious community, it makes sense that this triune God would long for something similar for his children. Given who God is, I think it's safe to trust that we will be supported in our wee attempts to build God-pleasing villages, or at least village-ettes.

Perhaps one of the most observable, if small, examples of this building process in my adult, still-single life has occurred over the last six years here in DC. It started off with a friend's brother moving to town. Jim was (and still is) handsome, and I couldn't help but wonder if he might be the knight sent to rescue this princess. But he wasn't interested in me in that way, and when I asked God about it, all I heard was, *Be kind and be real.* So I committed to relinquish my agenda (not easy to do, but possible), respect God's request, and practice being kind and real, whatever that meant. It turned out to mean playing some tennis, having some honest talks over Thai food, and offering genuinely mutual encouragement.

Over time, Jim started dating Cara, and she and I subsequently got to know each other. What was amazing was that my interactions with Cara became part of a larger conversation she was having with Jim and a few others about God. Somewhere along the line, Cara ended up embracing a faith in Jesus. I remember feeling awed knowing I'd been a part of her process. The reality of her newfound faith was so much more real and life-giving than my initial empty speculations about a rescuing knight.

Eventually, Jim and Cara married, and two years later they had Alex. Amazingly, they asked me to be Alex's godmother. This was a request not to be a fairy godmother but the real thing—the "I'll pray for you for the rest of your life and be there as much as I can" kind of godmother. I'd already made that commitment to one little boy, Silas, and knew how it had galvanized my relationship with him and his parents. So I said yes.

Jim, Cara, and I now have a tiny slice of community cemented with a permanent and shared purpose: Alex's well-being. Six years ago when this all began I could never have predicted such an outcome. And while the four of us don't live in Camelot (and I still would like a flesh-and-blood, if imperfect, knight), the periodic tastes of the village are real—we are people who can grill out, talk about real things, connect with one another's extended families, or just do nothing in each other's presence and enjoy it.

Maybe the final lesson in all of this, at least as far as I can see, is that community—even in an unraveling world with so many single people—is possible. It just might mean starting small with something as little as a newborn, as daunting as a drug-filled street, or as vulnerable as a personal need. We might have to risk tabling our fantasies and frustrations for a while and grabbing onto whatever bricks and mortar—whatever truth and love—we can get hold of and start building. Who knows, maybe with a real God who really wants his Kingdom of villages built, we will slowly see the least of us—fun-loving toddlers, that broken-down neighborhood, or a too-busy single woman—become a thousand. Maybe our small efforts will have mighty results. Maybe with his presence, his children can raise a village—or two.

CHAPTER 20

Homeward Bound

Recently, after eight months spent with a big purple iris on my screen saver, I began scrolling through other options. I came to one entitled "Home." It was a picture of a ruddy adobe wall with a deep-set, blue-framed window. Potted geraniums, desert wildflowers, and hot peppers hanging from a wooden ladder rounded out the picture. "Home," the computer called it. Home. Growing up on the East Coast, and spending most of my life amid red brick and big trees, adobe-style architecture does not connote "home" for me. Nevertheless, I wanted that picture as my screen saver, because in addition to its dynamic, contrasting colors, the picture reveals touches of beauty born from hard work. Geraniums don't pop into and out of pots spontaneously. Peppers don't magically grow and then hang themselves out to dry. Window frames don't paint themselves blue. It takes the presence of loving people to build a beautiful home. Looking at that picture stirred longings in me for that never-quite-fulfilled sense of home in my life.

I remember the first time I consciously longed for home. It snuck up on me when I was spending the night at my friend Sarah's house. As the sun went down and the night crept in, a shaky hollowness—not to be filled by any amount of TV or chocolate ice cream—took residence in my six-year-old stomach. Finally, as bedtime approached and my tears kept coming, Sarah's parents reluctantly called mine to come and pick me up (we lived about six blocks away). My parents came, and I think I probably slept happily ever after that night. How strange it was, then, to recognize echoes of that feeling so many years later.

Working for an urban nonprofit that embodied so much of what I sincerely (if idealistically) valued, I couldn't think of a better place to be as a thirty-year-old single woman. Well, almost. One night, while I was out to dinner with a cool friend, Leslie, in a chic Philadelphia café, that vaguely familiar feeling hit me with an appetite-numbing potency. We had been talking about Leslie's new apartment and how great it was that she could walk everywhere, decorate her own space, and have numerous friends stop by. I felt quite envious of her quintessential downtown life and readily confessed so. I had been feeling restless and thought it would help if I had my own hip, downtown place. But Leslie said that as much as she loved her apartment, she, too, had been feeling unsettled and didn't know why.

"Is it the man ache?" I ventured, referring to what I knew to be a common yearning among my single girlfriends and me.

"Possibly," she replied.

But bright and beautiful, Leslie had a solid handful of men, including a real "potential," chasing her. As we sat there, in between making observations about our somewhat affected waiter and some of the people we knew in common, we slowly explored the content of our restlessness: Leslie was really lonely for *what*? I thought getting my own hip, downtown apartment would bring me *what?* Finally, we stumbled upon a word that epitomized the object of our shared longing.

"This is going to sound kind of crazy, but I think I'm looking for *home,*" one of us said.

"Yes! That's it. *Home,*" the other agreed.

We were both about the same age, desirous of marriage, and also unabashedly enjoying our freedom to do whatever we wanted (like go out to dinners at chic cafés) whenever we wanted. Simultaneously, we were both hungering for some elusive sense of home that neither of us—great apartments and suitors notwithstanding—could find. We were both homesick.

Driving away from dinner that night, I intuitively knew that this grown-up homesickness was one from which neither my mom nor my dad, neither chic restaurants with cool friends nor my own apartment, nor even—as it took me much longer to accept—a "dream man," could rescue me. And that made me shudder.

I've realized since that night that the longing for home is not unique to any of us. The book of Hebrews speaks of those who were "aliens and strangers on earth . . . looking for a country of their own."[56] And songs, both old and new, are littered with references to home. I e-mailed one music-savvy girlfriend, Polly, about songs referencing home, and she instantly sent back a list of "classics," such as "Homeward Bound" (Simon & Garfunkel), "Country Roads" (John Denver), and "Sweet Home Alabama" (Lynyrd Skynyrd). Bruce Springsteen, U2, and Shawn Colvin have also done home-related songs, she reminded me.

I remember watching a local musical performed in an old rock quarry outside Lexington, Virginia. Entitled *Stonewall Country*, the musical is about the experience of Stonewall Jackson during the Civil War. One song, sung by soldiers on the field, has a haunting chorus that ends with this phrase: "Don't let me come home a stranger/ I couldn't stand to be a stranger."[57]

The timeless yearning for someplace called home and the fear of not being able to find it runs throughout the Civil War soldiers' song. One hundred and fifty years later and in a cultural milieu that those soldiers, Yankee or Confederate, never could have envisioned, I see those same concurrent yearnings and fears in myself and in the hearts of many single women I know. Sometimes I've wondered if the search for husband, kids, and a house is, in the soul of many of us, inextricably linked with the even deeper desire for something that is more than the simple sum of those parts. It is a search for *home*, for some intangibly warm and languid sense of permanent place and belonging.

I've also begun to wonder if perhaps one of the reasons singleness can take on particularly painful dimensions for some women is because it doesn't simply frustrate the desire for certain levels of intimacy (which it does). It goes beyond that and seems to be a shut door to the heart's yearning for home. It appears as if, by virtue of being single, one is automatically relegated to an emotional if not literal "homelessness," forced to perpetually live off the sparse handouts of others.

In his book *The Holy Longing*, Ronald Rolheiser goes so far as to say that sleeping alone gives a person a strange kinship with the poor. I think of Mary, a homeless woman who often lingers near the subway stop I frequent. Mary and I have had a number of conversations, and I am always taken aback by the sense of like-heartedness I feel with this admittedly bipolar bag lady. However, when I read Rolheiser's words, my experiences with Mary and other homeless acquaintances begin to make sense. He writes, "To sleep alone is to be poor. To sleep alone is to be stigmatized. To sleep alone is to be outside the norm for human intimacy and to acutely feel the sting of that."[58] Mary and I both feel our placelessness and longing for home. One time she asked me if I lived alone. When I explained that I had housemates, her response was emphatic and, because of that, poignant: "It's good you have friends. It's a terrible thing to be alone. I'm glad you have friends. I'm glad you're not alone."

The question remains, however: What will we do when we are aching, when we are homesick? What will we do when we discover that no fantasy knight, no ideal job, no chic lifestyle, no Pottery Barn digs, and no positive self-talk will completely rescue us? One option is to just keep eating chocolate ice cream and watching more *Friends* reruns or the History Channel in hopes of numbing out the homesickness. Alternatively, some of us might pour our discontent into anger at men's passivity, God's poorly exercised sovereignty, our own endless "issues," whatever (or whomever) else we can blame for our painful longings. If we're not careful, we can allow our legitimate hunger to drive us toward fruitless encounters with men, unhealthy expectations of friends, overinvestment in jobs that don't give back, hiding out, or hoarding more and more cash, hoping that one of these will be our ticket home. I have tried sips of most of these homesickness antidotes and know enough to know they aren't the cure.

There is another alternative, however. It is not an easy alternative, but it's straightforward enough. It is to simply let the ache work on us, shape us, and thereby do its job. When we let the ache become part of our story and not something to be conquered through striving or numbed by our narcotic of choice, it can serve us well. It can propel us forward, paradoxically, in life-giving—even joy-giving—ways. It can remind us that we are made for something more—that this life is not all it was intended to be—and it's good to want more. It can remind us that our longing for intimacy, connection, and home is real—it's part of our DNA, and it's nothing to be ashamed of. It can prompt us to look at our lives honestly and face current realities head-on. But most of all, if we can "walk with the ache, even when it hurts," as my friend Caroline likes to say, something amazing can occur.

We can receive with the ache the gift of standing face-to-face with fundamental questions that people have grappled with for aeons: What makes for a truly happy and satisfying life? And where is God in the midst of it all?

Sitting with those kinds of questions is scary. It's scary not just because unmet longings can feel almost physically painful, which they can. But more significantly, it can be scary to sit with those questions because we worry that the answers might be profoundly disappointing. What if a truly happy and satisfying life demands a husband or good sex or a sparkling career—and you are decidedly short on all three? Or what if ideas about a loving, trustworthy God were long ago deconstructed for you? And now, because you can't see or touch him, you fear there's no conclusion other than that he's, at best, just far away? Of course, we'll never be able to wade through our fears and questions if we don't risk facing them. And the ache can help us face them, if we'll let it.

When we do, we just might discover that this place of our fear is also the exact place where faith has a chance to show up. It is in the asking, in the midst of the fearful place, where we have the chance to believe and discover that some kind of *home* is out there, and it can be found by anyone, starting now.

Because I have friends from across the faith spectrum, I sometimes find it easiest to talk about God in general terms, which isn't all bad because there really is only one God. But here is where I have to branch away from what feels comfortable and say that as I've struggled with that ache, and as I've looked for faith, the center on which my faith has become lodged is Jesus. I'm talking about the historic, fleshly, earthly man who was also, as he claimed and as I've come to believe, the Son of God.

In a song made popular as the theme song for the TV show *Joan of Arcadia*, singer/songwriter Joan Osborne asks this question:

> *What if God was one of us?*
> *Just a slob like one of us*
> *Just a stranger on the bus*
> *Trying to make his way home*

I like this song not because I think Osborne is intentionally talking about Jesus; I don't. But the song gets at a funny little paradox that seems so universal: We desire God to be *with us* as we journey *toward him*. Somehow we know we're not there yet, but we want his real and human help in getting home.

In *The Message*, Eugene Peterson's rendition of the Bible, he translates a short portion of the book of John this way:

> *The Word became flesh and blood,*
> *and moved into the neighborhood.*
> *We saw the glory with our own eyes,*
> *the one-of-a-kind glory,*
> *like Father, like Son,*
> *Generous inside and out,*
> *true from start to finish.*[59]

I don't know that Jesus was a slob, but I do know that he was human, like all of us. Centuries ago, he moved into an actual neighborhood. In seeing him, in getting to know him, and in walking with him (which we do through the words of the Old and New Testaments, the strange adventure of prayer, and the stories and lives of a lot of friends), we can begin to make our way home. Or to put it another way, he enables us catch his same bus, to connect with God, his heavenly Father.

In humility, I must say that I don't really understand what I've just written nearly as much as I'd like. As a matter of fact, at certain points along the way—particularly during this journey of unintentional singleness—different aspects of Jesus' life, work, and purpose have taken various degrees of prominence in my mind and heart. I've not been able to boil it all down as much as some might hope.

Instead, sometimes I've focused on how in his death and resurrection, Jesus mysteriously took the penalty for what I called in an early chapter my identity fraud—my seeking to usurp God's role and, like a rebel queen, become Me Almighty. Because Jesus took my punishment, I'm able to bask in the freedom of not having to run and hide anymore. In spite of the sewer that has run through my life, I can show my face at home, because something—Someone—has been working on my behalf.

At other times, I've been struck by Jesus' life well lived. But that's not just because he is a good role model, though that's true. Beyond that, as Peterson's paraphrase puts it, in Jesus we see who God is, i.e., "like Father, like Son." So the compassion, the steely nerves, the big-picture vision, the tenderness toward the nobodies, the unwillingness to put up with lies, the desire for the comfort others bring, the love for his friends—all these traits (and these are just a few I've observed) are glimpses into what God is like. And while I know that whatever frame I create will always be too small, this evolving picture of God is alluring.

Lastly, though perhaps most significant for my daily life, I've repeatedly experienced the presence of Jesus that has remained in the world, even after he moved out of the neighborhood. When he was leaving, Jesus promised he'd send his Spirit, the Holy Spirit, to continue making his presence felt in the real, sloppy, messy lives of all kinds of people. So it's there, resident in the hearts of all kinds of people, the vast majority of whom I don't even know. I've seen this Spirit to be real, true from start to finish, showing up in the lives and stories of my friends. I've glimpsed a God whose Spirit enables people to embrace their talents and risk going new places; a God whose Spirit helps women and men get beyond all kinds of weirdness and relate to each other with authenticity and love; a God whose Spirit creates freedom, enables forgiveness, and helps people build communities from scratch. I've seen a God whose Spirit gives me the strength to be a genuinely joyful bridesmaid yet another time, and who leads me through a crazy culture when all the reliable maps seem to be missing. In short, I've seen a God who can take the achy, sometimes crushed grapes of my life and, hovering over the mess, transform it—transform me—into mighty fine wine.

I hope you've seen glimpses of that in your own life as well. So for now, I recognize my homesickness as something through which God's going to walk with me, in ways that I think will surprise me for the good. And when the ache is too much—when I just have to plop down on the floor and burst out crying—I'll again get his help to keep walking, realizing that homesickness is simply a reminder. My longings are in line with my design; I'm created for the secure joys of coming home.

When Jesus was preparing his followers for his departure, he spoke these words to them: "Do not let your hearts be troubled. Trust in God; trust also in me. In my Father's house are many rooms; if it were not so, I would have told you. I am going there to prepare a place for you. And if I go and prepare a place for you, I will come back and take you to be with me that you also may be where I am."[60]

In short, Jesus has gone on ahead to get the house ready for you, me, and a slew of other unknown-to-me people to come home. Maybe it's a strange concept to some folks, but something about this party grows increasingly amazing to me the more I travel. In the last book of the Bible, this homecoming is compared to a wedding and reception of celestial proportions. It's the marriage of Jesus and his people. Finally, after a very long wait, Jesus gets to be with those who've known him and those he has known, and we all find a place in the Father's home. That awes me.

Beyond that, I don't know what happens. Something about a new heaven and a new earth, I think. I suspect, though, that coming home is not just about settling down and curling up like a tired cat in front of a fire. Rather, as C. S. Lewis said, this life—the one where we're drinking coffee, laughing out loud, closing deals, meeting people, and sometimes aching in a busy, busy world—is simply the title page for the main story that is yet to come.[61] So, at least for today, I'm content to let that real story be revealed in its own time.

In the interim, whether I'm single or married, working at a meaningful job or just making some money, seeing community built or struggling with loneliness, enjoying the company of my friends or stretched far thinner than is healthy, I want to live out the advice of my friend Cheryl. Cheryl, whose ability to hold on to her honest desire for marriage (and the ache at the desire unmet) while still engaging the world of people and work in ways that amaze me, often says this: "Let's party," she declares, "till they see Jesus!" What a great image. If the party is what awaits us when we get home, then how great to start practicing it now. And given my understanding and what I've seen in the hearts of my friends, I might only offer this one addendum. "Let's party," I want to declare, "not just till the cows come home, but till everyone who wants to finally comes on home."

Notes

A Happy and Satisfying Life?

1 Jenny Norenberg, "I Can Do Anything, So How Do I Choose?" *Newsweek* (December 6, 2004): 18.

[2] Ibid.

[3] John 1:14, *The Message*.

An Uncharted Desert Isle

[4] Hebrews 11:8.

Our Many Selves

[5] See Luke 15:11-32.

Garden of the Heart

[6] Song of Songs 4:12.

I Just Gotta Be Queen

[7] Barbara Dafoe Whitehead, *Why There Are No Good Men Left: The Romantic Plight of the New Single Woman* (New York: Broadway Books, 2003), 76.

[8] Romans 7:15.

[9] C. S. Lewis, *The Weight of Glory* (New York: HarperCollins, 1949), 26.

[10] Whitehead, *Why There Are No Good Men Left*, 17.

[11] Frederica Mathewes-Green, *Gender: Men, Women, Sex, and Feminism* (Ben Lomond, Calif.: Conciliar Press, 2002).

Men—Who Needs Them?

[12] Whitehead quotes, on pages 172–173, from Ellen Fein and Sherrie Schneider, *The Rules: Time-Tested Secrets for Capturing the Heart of Mr. Right* (New York: Warner Books, 1995), 49.

[13] Genesis 1:27, NASB.

Freedom!

[14] "Brilliant Brandi," *CNN Sports Illustrated*, http://sportsillustrated.cnn.com/soccer/world/1999/womens_worldcup/news/1999/07/10/us_china_ap.

[15] Romans 8:9.

[16] Chris P. Rice, *Grace Matters* (San Francisco: Josey-Bass, 2002), 117.

[17] Psalm 16:6-7.

Not Gettin' It

[18] In all fairness, I don't know if Josh Harris's book *I Kissed Dating Goodbye* ultimately would have been relevant to my life or not. It seemed a little simplistic at the time, but it could have been that I was feeling unusually complex then!

[19] Ronald Rolheiser, *The Holy Longing: The Search for a Christian Spirituality* (New York: Doubleday, 1999), 7–8.

Gettin' It

[20] Paula Rinehart, *Sex and the Soul of a Woman* (Grand Rapids, Mich.: Zondervan, 2004), 92.

[21] Ibid., 90.

[22] Ibid., 89.

[23] Patricia Dalton, "Daughters of the Revolution: Too Many Young Women Have a Faulty Blueprint for What Liberation Means," *Washington Post* (May 21, 2000): B01.

[24] Genesis 3:1-6.

Girls Loving Girls

[25] Lori Rentzel, *Emotional Dependency: How to Keep Your Friendships Healthy* (Downers Grove, Ill.: InterVarsity Press, 1990), 89.

[26] Ibid., 18.

[27] John Piper, "The Other Dark Exchange—Homosexuality," http://www.desiringgod.org/library/sermons/98/101898.html.

[28] C. S. Lewis, *The Four Loves* (New York: Harcourt, 1960), 81–82.

[29] Deuteronomy 5:7-8.

[30] Rentzel, *Emotional Dependency*, 26.

[31] Exodus 33:11.

[32] Matthew 11:19.

[33] Lewis, *The Four Loves*, 126.

If Mama Ain't Happy . . .

[34] Victoria Secunda, *Women and Their Fathers* (New York: Delacorte Press, 1992), 100.

[35] Toni Morrison, *Beloved* (New York: Plume, 1993), 45.

Dads and Daughters

[36] Philippians 4:11-13, emphasis added.

So, Why Aren't You Married?

[37] Whitehead, *Why There Are No Good Men Left*, 25.

[38] John 9:2-3, *The Message*.

[39] John 9:3, NIV.

Dancing Shoes

[40] Michelle McKinney Hammond, *Sassy, Single, and Satisfied* (Eugene, Ore.: Harvest House, 2003).

[41] Jeremiah 31:3-4.

When Good Friends Marry Off

[42] Psalm 37:25.

Good Fences Make Good Neighbors

[43] Bill Clinton, *My Life* (New York: Knopf Publishing, 2004).

[44] Paula Rinehart, "The Price Tag of Sexual Indiscretions," *The News & Observer* (November 19, 2004), 166.

[45] Ibid.

[46] Ibid.

[47] John 17:24, emphasis added.

Work Part 1: Good-Bye, Fear

[48] See Matthew 25:14-30.

Work Part 2: Hello, Wisdom

[49] Frederick Buechner, *Wishful Thinking: A Theological ABC* (New York: Harper and Row, 1973), 95.

[50] Ibid.

[51] Proverbs 2:3-6, 9-10.

Where's the Village?

[52] Michael Ryan, "On the Nature of Poetry," in *Poetics*, ed. Paul Mariani and George Murphy (Green Harbor, Mass.: Tendril, 1984), 231–244.

[53] Robert D. Putnam, *Bowling Alone: The Collapse and Revival of American Community* (New York: Simon & Schuster, 2000).

[54] Isaiah 60:22.

[55] Psalm 127:1, RSV.

Homeward Bound

[56] Hebrews 11:13-14.

[57] Robin and Linda Williams, "Don't Let Me Come Home a Stranger," *Stonewall Country*.

[58] Rolheiser, *The Holy Longing*, 210.

[59] John 1:14.

[60] John 14:1-3.

[61] C. S. Lewis, *The Last Battle* (New York: HarperCollins, 1994), 228.

Acknowledgments

The joke among some of my friends is that it has taken more than a village to raise this child; rather, it has taken a concerted effort of folks across the nation! The same could be said about this book. I'd like to acknowledge the many people whom the faithful, loving, tri-une God (to whom I owe ultimate thanks) has used to help me write this book.

Thanks first to Pam Anderson and Dot Exum, both of whom gave me space—literally—to write. Pam gave me a home and an office, and Dot, a cabin to which I could escape. I am indebted to both of you. Thanks, too, to the International Student Ministries of the U.S. Navigators, who also provided some seriously subsidized office space along the way.

As well, I would like to thank the people who have prayed for me. I'm thinking of my prayer team, with special thanks to Jennifer Ennis, Elaine Harman, Elizabeth Harman Erickson, Sally Breedlove, Tracy Schutte, and Terri Merwin.

In addition, I would like to thank my many encouraging (and con-tributing) friends. Encouragers at the outset and along the way to whom I owe so much include Paula Rinehart (her advice and cheer-leading have been invaluable), Ann McCain, Jeanne Thum, Maria Graham, Ann Holladay, Pam and Bob Rowen-Herzog, Cheryl Meredith, Polly Hunter, Mary Ellen Barton, Karin Voth Harman, Glenn Lucke, Jerry and Jeannie Herbert, Jim and Cara Voth, and Joel and Dolly Woodruff.

As well, I owe many thanks to the women who have shared their stories with me: Ellen Merry, Cindi Slaughter, Lynn Gibson, Eleanor

Nagy, Nancy Clausen, Libby Conrad, Kristen Bucher, Gwen Griffith, Stephanie Bobb, Jana Polzin, Liz Woo, Abby Martin, Tracy Elizabeth Clay, Liz Kimberlin, Kelley Kenyan, Courtney Morrison, Karen Krispin, Kelli Donovan, Karen Coburn, Mary Ann Carter, Carol Weatherly, Rachel Kraines, Kristi Vera, Jen Goodson, and Karen Taniguchi. Your stories have shaped this book.

On a different note, I'd also like to thank my agent, Leslie Nunn Reed, and my editor from Tyndale, Lisa Jackson. Each of you provided much-needed personal enthusiasm for (and tightening up of) my writing. I'd like, too, to thank my colleagues with the Navigators for giving me the freedom to pursue this project.

Lastly, I'd like to thank my family. My brothers, Tom and Robert, and their families have given me the much-needed encouragement to believe that God is really in this. (Robert, thank you for the endless George MacDonald quotes.)

Of course, last but really first in so many ways are my parents, Tom and Diane Gilliam. You are loving, faithful, sharp, kind, committed, and so much fun. I love you, I'm grateful for all your love and support in this project, and as I've mentioned before: Without you, I wouldn't be. . . .

FREE DISCUSSION GUIDE!

A DISCUSSION GUIDE FOR

Revelations of a Single Woman

IS AVAILABLE AT

ChristianBookGuides.com

SaltRiver Books are a bit like saltwater:
Buoyant. Sometimes stinging. A mixture of sweet
and bitter, just like real life. Intelligent, thoughtful,
and finely crafted—but not pretentious, condescending,
or out of reach. They take on real life from a Christian
perspective. Look for SaltRiver Books, an imprint
of Tyndale House Publishers, everywhere
Christian books are sold.

www.saltriverbooks.com

SALT**RIVER**

INTELLIGENT. THOUGHT-PROVOKING. AUTHENTIC.

CONNALLY GILLIAM has lived the single experience. And by the grace of a good, unthreatened, big, and triune God, she has managed to move forward creatively, successfully, and sometimes painfully to navigate the world of unsought singleness.

Connally received her undergraduate degree in English literature from the University of Virginia, a diploma in Christian Studies from Regent College, and a master's of teaching in English from the University of Virginia.

Connally currently works in Washington, DC, with the U.S. Navigators as a "faith-based life coach" among twentysomethings. She loves playing tennis, drinking coffee with friends, and discovering how God is real, even in a crazy, changing, and unintentionally single world.